Level C

# Test Best® for Test Prep

## Teacher's Edition



STECK-VAUGHN
BERRENT
PUBLICATIONS



ISBN 0-8172-5840-X



1 2 3 4 5 6 7 8 9 0 03 02 01 00 99 98

# Contents

# About the Program

*Test Best® for Test Prep* has been developed to refresh basic skills, familiarize students with test formats and directions, and teach test-taking strategies for standardized tests. *Test Best* provides teachers with materials to ensure that students take the test under optimal conditions—that test-wise students be able to concentrate on what they know without being overwhelmed by a testing situation with which they are unfamiliar.

Being well prepared for a test means knowing how to approach different types of questions and how to use time wisely. By using the *Test Best* books prior to the administration of standardized tests, students will learn such skills, as well as be able to control their anxiety about a test and to keep their concentration high throughout the testing period. Armed with the skills they have learned as they work through *Test Best for Test Prep*, students can truly perform well.

**The *Test Best® for Test Prep* Series for Grades 2–8**

*Test Best for Test Prep* consists of seven student books. You will need to determine which book is best suited to the abilities and needs of your students. The series is organized as follows:

| Book | Grade Level |
|---|---|
| Level B | Grade 2 |
| Level C | Grade 3 |
| Level D | Grade 4 |
| Level E | Grade 5 |
| Level F | Grade 6 |
| Level G | Grade 7 |
| Level H | Grade 8 |

**Objectives of the Series**

To Increase Awareness of Test-Taking Strategies

Test-taking strategies should focus on four important test principles:

1. Time Use
   - Not spending too much time on any one question
   - Working rapidly but comfortably
   - Marking items to return to if time permits
   - Using any time remaining to review answers
   - Using a watch (at the appropriate age) to keep track of time
2. Error Avoidance
   - Paying careful attention to directions
   - Determining clearly what is being asked
   - Marking answers in the appropriate place
   - Checking all answers
   - Avoiding making stray marks on the answer sheet
3. Reasoning
   - Reading the entire question or passage and all the choices before answering a question
   - Applying what has been learned
4. Guessing
   - Answering all the questions in the test within the allotted time.
   - Trying to eliminate known incorrect answer choices before guessing

To Increase Awareness of Directions

It is important that students understand the directions for taking the tests. Therefore, one of the key objectives of the program is to familiarize students with directions. Doing so builds self-confidence and permits students to utilize their time more effectively.

To Increase Awareness of Content and Skills

Anxiety often results from a lack of information about the knowledge and skills the tests will cover. You and your students will find that increased awareness of content and skills are significant outcomes of the program.

To Increase Awareness of Format

By practicing the skills needed to meet your school's educational objectives, the students will gain invaluable experience with test formats. Such familiarity permits students to spend more time applying what they have learned.

To Understand How the Test Is Administered

Students are sometimes uncomfortable anticipating what will happen on the day of the tests. Becoming familiar with the procedures, directions, and the process of test taking helps reduce anxiety and uncertainty.

**Format of the Books**

Each of the seven student books is divided into units that correspond to those found on standardized tests. The units include Reading Comprehension, Reading Vocabulary, Mathematics Problem Solving and Procedures, Listening, and Language. Within each of these units are the skills covered on the tests.

Each skill lesson generally includes:

Directions—clear, concise, and similar to those found in most standardized tests;

Try This—A skill strategy for students that enables them to approach each lesson exercise in a logical manner;

A Sample—to familiarize students with test-taking items;

Think It Through—a specific explanation to students of the correct answer in the Sample item that tells why the correct answer is correct and why the incorrect answers are wrong.

A Practice Section—a set of exercises based on the lesson and modeled on the kinds of test items found in standardized tests.

Each unit is followed by a Unit Test that covers all the skills in the unit lessons and affords students the opportunity to experience a situation close to the testing situation. Each book concludes with a series of five Comprehensive Tests. The *Test Best* Comprehensive Tests give students an opportunity to take a test under conditions that parallel those they will face when taking standardized tests.

**The Teacher's Edition**

The Teacher's Edition of *Test Best for Test Prep* contains a Scope and Sequence and reduced student pages complete with answers. The Teacher's Edition also provides a detailed plan of action and suggestions for teaching and administering each of the lessons and tests, including Sample items. Scripts are provided so that students become familiar with oral directions given on the tests themselves.

Also contained in the Teacher's Edition is an introductory lesson designed to acquaint students with the *Test Best for Test Prep* program. This lesson appears on pages 6 through 8 and should be used before beginning Unit 1 with students.

# Scope and Sequence

**READING SKILLS**

| READING SKILLS | Unit 2: Reading Comprehension | Modeled Instruction | Unit 3: Reading Comprehension | Reading Selections | Unit 3 Test | PRACTICE TEST 1 | Unit 4: Reading Vocabulary | Understanding Word Meanings | Matching Words with More Than One Meaning | Using Context Clues | Unit 4 Test | PRACTICE TEST 2 | Unit 7: Listening | Listening for Word Meanings | Building Listening Skills | Unit 7 Test | PRACTICE TEST 4 |
|---|---|---|---|---|---|---|---|---|---|---|---|---|---|---|---|---|---|
| Identifying synonyms | | | | | | | | ■ | | | ■ | ■ | | | | | |
| Using sentence context to determine word meaning of multiple-meaning words | | ■ | | | | | | | ■ | | ■ | ■ | | | | | |
| Using sentence context to determine word meaning | | ■ | | | | | | | | ■ | ■ | ■ | | | | | |
| Understanding explicitly stated details, actions, reasons, sequence of events | | ■ | | ■ | ■ | ■ | | | | | | | | | | | |
| Making inferences | | ■ | | ■ | ■ | ■ | | | | | | | | | ■ | ■ | ■ |
| Inferring meaning | | ■ | | ■ | ■ | ■ | | | | | | | | | | | |
| Extending meaning | | ■ | | ■ | ■ | ■ | | | | | | | | | ■ | ■ | ■ |
| Making predictions | | ■ | | ■ | ■ | ■ | | | | | | | | | | | |
| Understanding implicit ideas | | ■ | | ■ | ■ | ■ | | | | | | | | | | | |
| Identifying author's purpose | | ■ | | ■ | ■ | ■ | | | | | | | | | | | |
| Using definitional phrases to determine word meaning | | ■ | | | | | | | | | | | | ■ | | ■ | ■ |
| Recalling details and sequence | | | | | | | | | | | | | | | ■ | ■ | ■ |
| Drawing conclusions | | | | | | | | | | | | | | | ■ | ■ | ■ |

# Scope and Sequence

| MATHEMATICS SKILLS | Unit 5: Math Problem-Solving Strategies | Using the Problem-Solving Plan | Unit 6: Math Problem Solving | Understanding Numeration | Using Whole Numbers, Fractions, and Decimals | Understanding Patterns and Relationships | Working With Statistics and Probability | Understanding Geometry | Working with Measurement | Solving Problems | Unit 6 Test | Math Procedures | Understanding Computation | Using Computation | Unit 6 Test | PRACTICE TEST 3 |
|---|---|---|---|---|---|---|---|---|---|---|---|---|---|---|---|---|
| Identifying odd and even numbers | | | | ■ | | | | | | | ■ | | | | | ■ |
| Recognizing numerals | | | | ■ | | | | | | | ■ | | | | | ■ |
| Understanding place value | | | | ■ | | | | | | | ■ | | | | | ■ |
| Comparing and ordering numbers | | | | ■ | | | | | | | ■ | | | | | ■ |
| Understanding families of number facts and the properties of whole numbers | | | | | ■ | | | | | | ■ | | | | | ■ |
| Understanding fundamental operations and fractional parts | | | | | ■ | | | | | | ■ | | | | | ■ |
| Comparing and ordering fractions and decimals | | | | | ■ | | | | | | ■ | | | | | ■ |
| Recognizing and interpreting number patterns and geometric patterns | | ■ | | | | ■ | | | | | ■ | | | | | ■ |
| Reading and interpreting bar graphs, tables, and tally charts | | | | | | | ■ | | | | ■ | | | | | ■ |
| Determining simple probability | | | | | | | ■ | | | | ■ | | | | | ■ |
| Recognizing geometric shapes | | | | | | | | ■ | | | ■ | | | | | ■ |
| Understanding basic properties of plane figures and rotations | | | | | | | | ■ | | | ■ | | | | | ■ |
| Identifying congruent figures and common solid figures | | | | | | | | ■ | | | ■ | | | | | ■ |
| Identifying units of measurement | | | | | | | | | ■ | | ■ | | | | | ■ |
| Measuring and comparing time and length using standard and nonstandard measurement units | | | | | | | | | ■ | | ■ | | | | | ■ |
| Determining the value of currency | | ■ | | | | | | | ■ | | ■ | | | | | ■ |
| Understanding currency exchange | | | | | | | | | ■ | | ■ | | | | | ■ |
| Determining solution sentences for fundamental operations | | | | | | | | | | ■ | ■ | | | | | ■ |
| Identifying missing information | | | | | | | | | | ■ | ■ | | | | | ■ |
| Using estimation in problem solving | | | | | | | | | | ■ | ■ | | | | | ■ |
| Identifying reasonableness | | | | | | | | | | ■ | ■ | | | | | ■ |
| Solving problems using logic | | ■ | | | | | | | | ■ | ■ | | | | | ■ |
| Adding, subtracting, multiplying, and dividing whole numbers | | | | | | | | | | | | | ■ | | ■ | ■ |
| Rounding | | | | | | | | | | | | | | ■ | ■ | ■ |
| Adding and subtracting whole numbers, decimals, and money in context | | ■ | | | | | | | | | | | | ■ | ■ | ■ |
| Multiplying whole numbers in context | | | | | | | | | | | | | | ■ | ■ | ■ |

# Scope and Sequence

**LANGUAGE SKILLS**

| LANGUAGE SKILLS | Unit 8: Language | Prewriting, Composing, Editing | Identifying Misspelled Words | Unit 8 Test | PRACTICE TEST 5 |
|---|---|---|---|---|---|
| Identifying appropriate sources of information | | ■ | | ■ | ■ |
| Using parts of a book to locate information | | ■ | | ■ | ■ |
| Determining appropriate prewriting activities | | ■ | | ■ | ■ |
| Alphabetizing words | | ■ | | ■ | ■ |
| Understanding dictionary entries | | ■ | | ■ | ■ |
| Evaluating prewriting strategies | | ■ | | ■ | ■ |
| Determining the relevance of ideas | | ■ | | ■ | ■ |
| Determining the purpose for writing | | ■ | | ■ | ■ |
| Evaluating importance of ideas | | ■ | | ■ | ■ |
| Recognizing well-constructed sentences | | ■ | | ■ | ■ |
| Recognizing correctly combined sentences | | ■ | | ■ | ■ |
| Identifying topic sentences in paragraphs | | ■ | | ■ | ■ |
| Identifying appropriate topic and concluding sentences | | ■ | | ■ | ■ |
| Recognizing sentence fragments | | ■ | | ■ | ■ |
| Identifying the correct tense of verbs | | ■ | | ■ | ■ |
| Using correct punctuation | | ■ | | ■ | ■ |
| Using correct capitalization | | ■ | | ■ | ■ |
| Understanding subject-verb agreement in number | | ■ | | ■ | ■ |
| Identifying misspelled words in sentences | | | ■ | ■ | ■ |

UNIT FOUR

## Reading Vocabulary

### Understanding Word Meanings

Directions: Darken the circle for the word or words that have the same or almost the same meaning as the underlined word, or write in the answer.

**TRY THIS** Choose your answer carefully. The other choices may seem correct. Be sure to think about the meaning of the underlined word.

Sample A

A check is a kind of—

Ⓐ box
Ⓑ picture
Ⓒ dance
● mark

**THINK IT THROUGH** The correct answer is D, mark. A check is a kind of mark. A check is not a box, a picture, or a dance.

STOP

1 Slender means—

Ⓐ quick
Ⓑ shy
● thin
Ⓓ lost

2 What is an ache?

*pain*

3 A cap is a kind of—

Ⓕ lock
● hat
Ⓗ head
Ⓙ coat

4 To connect is to—

Ⓐ hit
Ⓑ shut
● join
Ⓓ belong

5 Savage means—

Ⓕ hungry
● wild
Ⓗ comfortable
Ⓙ large

6 To oppose something is to—

Ⓐ cheer for it
● be against it
Ⓒ leave it
Ⓓ want it

STOP



48

## Introducing Students to *Test Best*®

Use this orientation lesson to familiarize students with the format of *Test Best for Test Prep, Level C*, and with steps for preparing for and taking standardized tests.

SAY: **At certain times during the school year, you may take one or more special tests. These tests show how well you are doing in certain subjects, compared with other students of your age group across the country. Some test questions will be harder than others, and some may be new to you. But that's all right. You will be given enough time to work on each test.**

Distribute the *Test Best* books to students. Tell students that *Test Best* will use the same kinds of questions that are found on standardized tests. Using the books will be practice for taking the special test. Allow students to skim through the books for a minute or two. Circulate around the room, making sure that all students are turned to the correct page as you examine the books.

SAY: **Now we will look at one of the lessons. Turn to Unit 4 on page 48. Notice that this page has *Unit 4, Reading Vocabulary*, at the top of the page. This tells you the number and the name of the unit. This unit is about words. Just under the unit number and name it has *Understanding Word Meanings*. That tells you the name of the lesson. This lesson is about words and what they mean. This is how a lesson page looks.**

Ask students if they have any questions.

SAY: **Put your finger on the Directions.**

Explain that each lesson begins with a set of Directions. Read the Directions aloud. Ask students why it is important to read and follow directions when taking tests.

SAY: **Find the Try This section. Let's read this section together. Try This suggests a way to answer the question. There are other ways to figure the answer to a question. Try This offers one way. Now look at the Sample below Try This. We will always work through the Sample together before you work the practice exercises on your own.**

Copy the Sample onto the chalkboard. Work through the Sample orally with students, and demonstrate the proper way to darken the answer spaces. Explain to students the importance of filling the answer space, pressing firmly with the pencil to make a dark mark, and erasing any stray marks that might be picked up as answers by the scoring machines.

## Test

**Directions: Read each story carefully. Then read each question. Darken the circle for the correct answer, or write in the answer.**

**TRY THIS** — **More than one answer choice may sound correct. Choose the answer that goes best with the story.**

Sample A **Kangaroos**

Kangaroos come in all sizes. The smallest kangaroo is the musky rat. It is about six inches tall. The largest kangaroo is the red kangaroo. It is about six feet tall. It lives in the dry central part of Australia. Red kangaroos are great jumpers.

**How tall is a musky rat?**

Ⓐ about six feet

Ⓑ about six centimeters

● about six inches

Ⓓ very tiny

**THINK IT THROUGH** — **The correct answer is C, about six inches. The third sentence in the story contain this information.**

STOP

### The Great Sphinx

The Egyptians made statues of sphinxes to honor kings or queens. A sphinx has the head of a human and the body of a lion. The oldest and largest sphinx is the Great Sphinx. It was built in the desert near Giza, Egypt, thousands of years ago. It is 240 feet long and 66 feet high. At times the Great Sphinx has been buried by sand. Weather has worn away part of the stone. Today scientists are working on ways to save the Great Sphinx. They hope special chemicals will keep it from crumbling.

1 **Why was the Great Sphinx built?**

● to honor a king or queen

Ⓑ to honor lions

Ⓒ to protect Giza, Egypt

Ⓓ to attract tourists

2 **How do scientists plan to save the Great Sphinx?**

***by using special chemicals to keep it from crumbling***

GO ON





SAY: **Now find Think It Through. Think It Through is an explanation of the best answer. Think It Through usually explains why the other choices are wrong.**

Read Think It Through to students. Ask students if they have any questions about the lesson features up to this point.

SAY: **What do you see below Think It Through and at the bottom of the page? (A stop sign) What should you do when you see a stop sign? (Stop what you are doing.)**

Tell students that they will see the stop sign throughout the lessons and on standardized tests. Explain that a stop sign tells students to stop what they are doing, put their pencils down, and wait for further instructions from the teacher.

SAY: **What do you see below Think It Through and the stop sign? (Numbered exercises) Each lesson has a practice section with exercises. When you decide on your answer, you will use your pencil to darken the circle, or answer space, for the correct answer choice.**

Ask students if they have any questions about the lesson page.

SAY: **Now turn to page 41 in your books. You should be on the page with the word *Test* at the top of the page.**

Make sure that all students find page 41. Explain that there is a unit test at the end of each unit that gives students an opportunity to practice taking a test. Tell students to look at page 41. Tell students that this is the unit test for the reading unit. Have students locate the Sample on the test. Tell students that you will always work the samples together as a class. Explain that the unit test will include the skills you have practiced together in the unit lessons.

SAY: **Now look at the bottom of page 41. What do you see at the right, just below question 2? (An arrow with the words *GO ON*) This tells you go to the next page.**

Tell students that in the *Test Best* book and on the standardized tests they will see the arrow with the words *GO ON*.

Ask students if they have any questions about the unit tests.

UNIT TEN

# Practice Test 2

## Reading Vocabulary

Sample A

A parka is a kind of—

● warm jacket with a hood

Ⓑ European folk dance

Ⓒ dried meat

Ⓓ sled

STOP

For questions 1-9, darken the circle for the word or words that have the same or almost the same meaning as the underlined word.

1 Familiar means—

Ⓐ old

Ⓑ beautiful

● known

Ⓓ strange

2 A lane is most like a—

Ⓕ ladder

● road

Ⓗ shack

Ⓙ race

3 To cure means to—

● heal

Ⓑ clean

Ⓒ study

Ⓓ correct

4 A tourist is a kind of—

Ⓕ judge

Ⓖ chair

Ⓗ teacher

● visitor

5 To recall something is to—

Ⓐ prepare it

Ⓑ clean it

● remember it

Ⓓ include it

6 Something that is precise is—

Ⓕ expensive

● exact

Ⓗ rare

Ⓙ safe

7 Something that is soaked is—

● wet

Ⓑ dirty

Ⓒ soiled

Ⓓ wrinkled

8 A jacket is most like a—

Ⓕ hat

Ⓖ dress

● coat

Ⓙ jar

9 A kennel is a place for—

● dogs

Ⓑ airplanes

Ⓒ plants

Ⓓ cars

STOP



105

SAY: **Now turn to page 105 in your books. You should be on the page with *Unit 10, Practice Test 2: Reading Vocabulary* at the top of the page.**

Make sure that all students find page 105. Explain that there are Comprehensive Tests at the end of the book. Tell students that the Comprehensive Tests are just like standardized tests.

SAY: **There are five Comprehensive Tests—one test for each unit in the book. When we take the Comprehensive Tests, we will follow the test conditions that will be used during standardized tests. For example, I will provide you with sharpened pencils. I will guide you during the tests and give you directions for each part of each test. The Comprehensive Tests will give you a final chance to apply the skills that you practiced in the lessons in Test Best before you take standardized tests.**

Ask students if they have any questions about the Comprehensive Tests.

SAY: **Now look at the bottom of page 105. What do you see at the right, just below number 9? (A stop sign) What does the stop sign tell you to do? (Stop what you are doing, put your pencils down, and wait for further instructions from the teacher.)**

Ask students if they have any questions about the Comprehensive Tests.

SAY: **When you take standardized tests, you may feel a little nervous at first. Try to remember what you have learned in Test Best about taking tests. You will be able to use what you have learned in your class, too. Then you should be ready to do your very best.**

UNIT ONE

# Reading: Test-Taking Strategies

The following strategies will help you do your best on standardized reading tests. These three strategies will assist you in organizing the information needed to successfully answer the questions.

## STRATEGY 1

**The CHECK AND SEE Strategy**
This strategy can be used when a question asks for a fact from the story. The answer to the question is right there in the story. It is not hidden. Some of the same words may be in the story and in the question.

**Check and See** will help you answer *remembering information* questions.

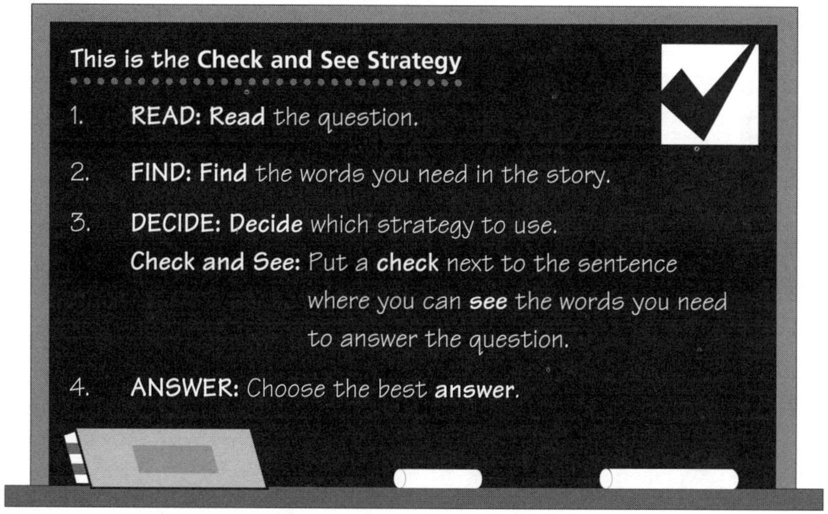


GO ON





## Unit 1 Reading: Test-Taking Strategies

Reading Strategies: The Check and See Strategy, the Puzzle Piece Strategy, and the What Lights Up Strategy

SAY: **Turn to Unit 1, Reading: Test Taking Strategies, on page 3.**

Check to see that all students find Unit 1.

SAY: **In Unit 1 you will read about three test-taking strategies that will help you answer questions about the stories that you read.**

Read the first paragraph to students.

SAY: **Now look at Strategy 1.**

Read the Check and See Strategy to students.

SAY: **Now look at what is written on the blackboard chart on page 3. Read the four steps silently.**

Review the strategy with students. Discuss with the class how this can help them answer reading comprehension questions when the answer is stated in the story.

## STRATEGY 2

**The PUZZLE PIECE Strategy**

This strategy can be used when a question asks you what something means. Sometimes there does not seem to be an answer. It is not stated in the story.

**Puzzle Piece** is the strategy to use when you must fit facts together to get the answer. This is like putting a puzzle together. Puzzles are made up of many pieces. You cannot look at one piece and know what the picture is. Only when you put the pieces together can you see the whole picture.

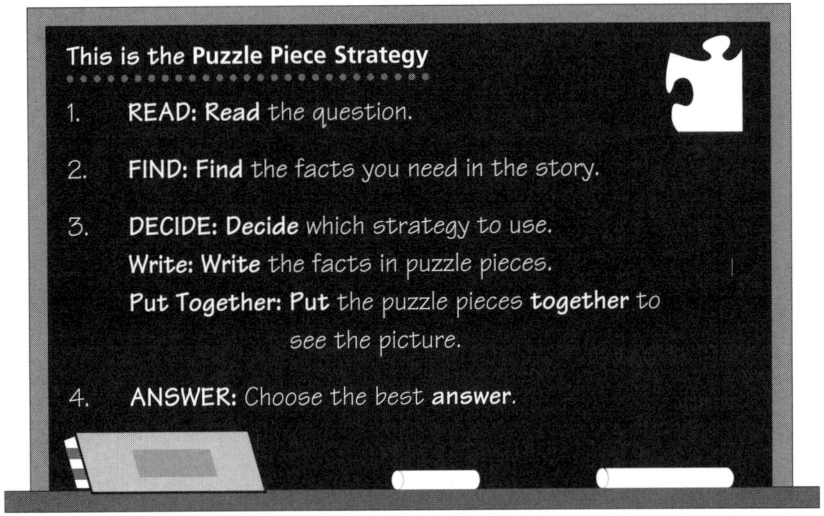




GO ON



SAY: **Now look at Strategy 2 on page 4.**

Read the Puzzle Piece Strategy to students.

SAY: **Now look at what is written on the blackboard chart on page 4. Read the four steps silently.**

Review the strategy with students. Discuss with the class how this can help them answer reading comprehension questions when the answer is not stated in the story.

### STRATEGY 3

**The WHAT LIGHTS UP Strategy**
This is another strategy you can use when an answer is not in the story. To answer the question you need to add your own ideas to the story. This added information can come from your own experiences.

**What Lights Up** can help you see if something is true, real, useful, or a fact. It can help you see what would happen if the story had a different ending.

You can use the **What Lights Up Strategy** to answer the hardest type of question. This is when you are asked to read and think of your own ideas. These questions are called *evaluating* and extending meaning questions.

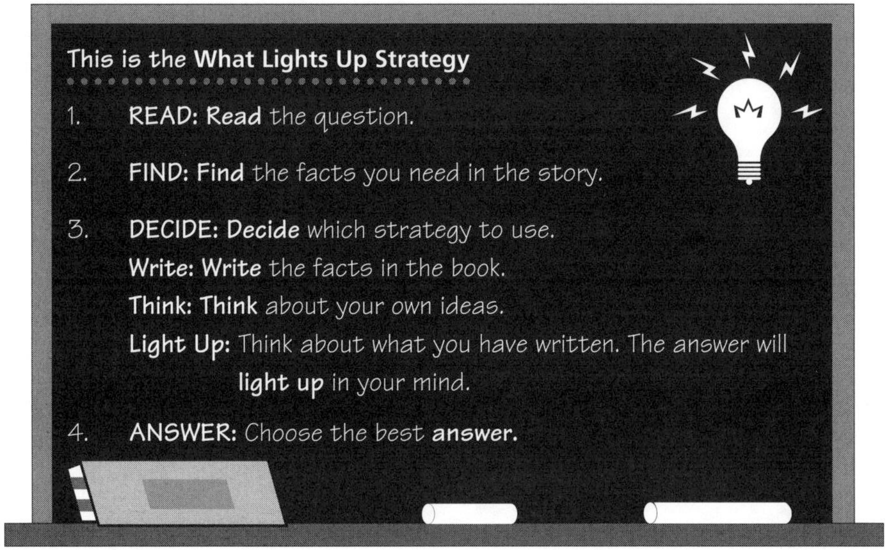




GO ON



SAY: **Now look at Strategy 3 on page 5.**

Read the What Lights Up Strategy to students.

SAY: **Now look at what is written on the blackboard chart on page 5. Read the four steps silently.**

Review the strategy with students. Discuss with the class how this can help them answer reading comprehension questions that ask them to write about something that is not found in the story.

UNIT TWO

# Reading Comprehension

Modeled Instruction

## Specific Objectives

**Objective 1: Determining word meanings**
*Prefixes and suffixes, context clues, technical words, and words with multiple meanings*

**Objective 2: Identifying supporting ideas**
*Recalling facts and details, sequential order, following directions, and describing settings*

**Objective 3: Summarizing main ideas**
*Stated and implied main ideas, and identifying summaries*

**Objective 4: Perceiving relationships and recognizing outcomes**
*Cause-and-effect and making predictions*

**Objective 5: Making inferences and generalizations**
*Interpreting graphs and diagrams, inferring information, drawing conclusions, making judgments, and evaluating plot*

**Objective 6: Recognizing points of view, facts, and opinions**
*Author's purpose, persuasive language, and discerning facts and points of view*





# Unit 2: Reading Comprehension Modeled Instruction

## Specific Objectives

The objectives on page 6 are intended to provide an overview of the material covered in Unit 2. The six objectives correlate with the reading and vocabulary skills covered throughout *Test Best for Test Prep*, as outlined in the Scope and Sequence chart found on page 3 of the Teacher's Edition.

## Modeled Instruction

### Objective 1: Determining Word Meanings

**Prefixes and suffixes are parts of some words. A *prefix* is at the start of a word. A *suffix* is at the end of a word. You can use prefixes and suffixes to figure out the meaning of a word.**

Whenever Shaquana invited a friend to sleep over, she made sure it was someone who liked to stay up late and tell scary stories. Lately, the only books Shaquana liked to read were about the supernatural.

1 **In this paragraph, the word supernatural means —**

- ● ghosts and spirits.
- Ⓑ people who really like nature.
- Ⓒ heroes.
- Ⓓ strong people.

*Hint: Read the entire paragraph. The prefix "super-" means* above or greater than normal.

Sometimes having an older sister drives me crazy. She plays her music really loud while I'm doing my homework. If I ask her to turn it down, she'll make it louder.

2 **In this paragraph, the word louder means —**

- Ⓕ quieter.
- ● more than loud.
- Ⓗ almost as loud.
- Ⓙ almost the same as it was before.

*Hint: The suffix "-er" means* more than.

Jeff went into his room to find his sneakers. Just as he got near his closet, he found that he was in darkness.

3 **What is meant by darkness?**

***There was no light in the room.***

*Hint: The suffix "-ness" means* a state of being.



GO ON



# Modeled Instruction

# Objective 1: Determining Word Meanings

Reading Skills: Identifying prefixes and suffixes, using context clues, and defining specialized or technical words

SAY: **Turn to Objective 1, Determining Word Meanings, on page 7.**

Check to see that all students find page 7.

SAY: **In this lesson you will practice answering questions about determining word meanings.**

Read the Directions to students.

SAY: **Now look at the paragraph that begins with the words *prefixes* and *suffixes.***

Read the paragraph to students.

SAY: **Now look at the first passage. Read the passage silently. Then answer the question that follows. *What does the word supernatural mean?* Darken the circle for the correct answer. Read the hint to help you answer the question.**

Allow students time to find and mark their answer.

SAY: **The correct answer is A. Supernatural means "ghosts and spirits." The prefix *super-* means "above" or "greater than normal."**

Check to see that all students have filled in the correct answer space. Ask students if they have any questions.

The girls were trying to remember what the new girl at camp was like. Joan said she had brown hair and was skinny. Phyllis thought she was on the tallish side.

**4 In this paragraph, the word tallish means —**

- Ⓐ that the new girl talked a lot.
- Ⓑ that the new girl was shy.
- ● that the new girl was rather tall.
- Ⓓ that the new girl was of Irish background.

*Hint: The suffix "-ish" means* somewhat or rather.

My mother asked me to get everything ready. She wanted to make dinner for us when she got home. She told me to take the meat out of the refrigerator and preheat the oven. Then she wanted me to start washing the lettuce.

**5 In this paragraph, the word preheat means —**

- Ⓕ check the temperature of.
- Ⓖ turn on.
- ● heat beforehand.
- Ⓙ clean.

*Hint: "Pre-" is a prefix. "Pre-" means* before.

The boys were planning a garage sale. They had cleaned the toys and found all the pieces for the games. But their old clothes were in such bad shape, they did not think they could resell them.

**6 What does it mean when someone resells something?**

***to sell again***

*Hint: "Re-" is a prefix. "Re-" means* to do something again.



GO ON



SAY: **Now you will practice answering questions about determining word meanings. Beginning on page 7, read each passage carefully and answer the questions that follow. Darken the circle for the correct answer, or write your answer in the space provided. Answer all the questions on pages 7 through 12. The information at the top of each page will tell you what to look for, and the hints after each question will help you determine the correct answer. When you come to the words *GO ON* at the bottom of a page, continue working on the next page. When you come to the word *STOP* at the bottom of page 12, put your pencils down. You may now begin.**

Allow students time to find and write their answers.

Review the questions and answer choices with students. Discuss with the class why one answer is correct and the others are not correct. Also check to see that students have carefully filled in their answer spaces and have completely erased any stray marks.

## Objective 1: Determining Word Meanings

**Sometimes you can figure out the meaning of a new word by using the words around it as clues.**

Sherlock Holmes is a great detective. But he lives only in books. The tales about him have been written in 57 languages.

1 **In this paragraph, the word tales means —**

Ⓐ places.

Ⓑ names.

● stories.

Ⓓ pens.

*Hint: You get a clue as to what the word* tales *means by reading sentences 2 and 3.*

Marie did not know how to operate the compact disc player. She read the manual. She hoped she could find the information she needed in the book.

2 **In this paragraph, the word manual means —**

Ⓕ a dictionary.

Ⓖ a compact disc.

Ⓗ a recipe book.

● a how-to book.

*Hint: You get a clue as to what the word* manual *means from the sentence after the one in which the word appears.*

Mother ducks often take their ducklings swimming. When a pond is full of mothers and babies, the mother ducks quack and swim around. Whichever mother duck quacks the loudest gets the greatest number of ducklings to swim around her.

3 **What are ducklings?**

***baby ducks***

*Hint: You get a clue as to what the word* ducklings *means from the second sentence in the paragraph.*



GO ON

Pat grew up wanting to be a postmaster. As a boy, whenever he went to the post office in his home town in Ohio, he would dream of running it. When he finished school, his dream almost came true. He became a postmaster, but in a different town in Ohio.

4 **In this paragraph, the word postmaster means —**

- Ⓐ someone who likes to collect stamps.
- Ⓑ an expert about postage.
- ● a person in charge of a post office.
- Ⓓ the person who posts time for runners.

*Hint: You get a clue as to what the word* postmaster *means from the sentence that tells about Pat's dream.*

Birds perch on a tree even while they sleep. Their toes grab the branch so they don't fall. Three toes point forward. One toe points backward. The toes lock tightly onto the branch.

5 **In this paragraph, the word perch means —**

- Ⓕ fly.
- ● sit.
- Ⓗ vanish.
- Ⓙ promise.

*Hint: You get a clue as to what the word* perch *means by reading the sentences after the one in which the word is.*

Doctors studied thousands of people. Some of the people spent a lot of time alone. Many of these people had weak hearts. They were more likely to have a heart attack. Other people spent a lot of time with their families and friends. Most of these social people had strong hearts.

6 **Describe someone who is social.**

***A person who is social is someone who spends a lot of time with his family and friends.***

*Hint: You get a clue as to what the word* social *means by reading the sentence before the word.*



GO ON

## Objective 1: Determining Word Meanings

**Specialized or technical words are used in science and social studies. You can use the other information in the passage to help figure out the meaning of these words.**

Sometimes, deep in the ocean, an earthquake shakes the ocean floor. The movement starts a tidal wave. At first, the wave is small. But it can move toward the shore at a speed of up to 500 miles per hour. By the time it reaches the coast, it is huge and hits hard.

1 **In this paragraph, tidal wave means —**

Ⓐ a way of saying hello.

● a very big wave sent to shore by an earthquake.

Ⓒ a strong gust of wind.

Ⓓ a group of people that stand up and down in a stadium.

*Hint:* Tidal wave *is a technical word. You get a clue as to what it means by reading the entire paragraph.*

There are giant ships more than 700 feet long. These ships were built to carry tons of wheat from place to place. They have a ramp folded up in back. When they get to shore, the ramp unfolds. The cargo is moved off the ship by the ramp.

2 **In this paragraph, the word cargo means —**

Ⓕ truck.

Ⓖ garbage.

● shipment.

Ⓙ flower.

*Hint:* Cargo *is a technical word. You get a clue as to what it means by reading the sentences before the word.*

Saliva helps you swallow food by making your throat slippery. Saliva softens food so that the tongue can taste it. Saliva also helps your body break down food.

3 **What is saliva and where do you find it?**

***Saliva is something that is found in your throat. It helps you swallow food, softens your food so your tongue can taste it and helps your body to break the food down.***

*Hint:* Saliva *is a technical word. You can get a clue as to what it means by reading the entire paragraph.*



GO ON

Wildflowers grow in many environments. Some are found in woods or fields. Others grow on mountains or in streams and ponds. Wildflowers can grow in the desert, too.

4 **In this paragraph, the word environments means —**

Ⓐ blossoms.

● settings.

Ⓒ oceans.

Ⓓ insects.

*Hint: You get a clue as to what* environments *means from the sentences after the word.*

Ted couldn't believe that he was on a real television set. Carpenters were working all around him building the scenes where the action would take place. Some painters were working on the rooms of a house, and others were painting a yard. He hoped his parents would let him stay long enough to meet one of the actors or actresses.

5 **In this paragraph, the word set means —**

Ⓕ a number of tools that are used together.

Ⓖ the number of couples needed for a square dance.

Ⓗ a group of tennis games.

● a place where a show is filmed.

*Hint:* Set *is a technical word. You get a clue as to what it means by reading the entire paragraph.*

Piranhas are fish. They live in South American waters. These fish tend to swim in large groups. They will tear the flesh off an animal or person that is in the water. In just minutes, all that is left is the skeleton.

6 **What is a skeleton?**

***An animal's or person's bones.***

*Hint:* Skeleton *is a technical word. You get a clue as to what it means by reading the sentence before the word.*



STOP

## Objective 2: Identifying Supporting Ideas

**Facts or details are important. By noticing them, you will know what the passage is about.**

The United States Supreme Court is the highest court of the land. For many years, only men were Supreme Court judges. That was true until 1981. That year, Sandra Day O'Connor became a Supreme Court judge. She was the first woman to do so.

Sandra's first teacher was her mother. Later, Sandra went to school. Sandra finished high school when she was just 16. Then, she followed her dream to study law. She was in law school for five years. When she finished law school, she couldn't find a job. Very few companies wanted women lawyers!

1 **Only men served on the Supreme Court —**

- Ⓐ after 1990.
- Ⓑ after 1811.
- Ⓒ until 1981.
- ● until 200 years ago.

*Hint: Look at sentences 2 and 3.*

2 **The highest court of the United States is the —**

- ● World Court.
- Ⓖ State Court.
- Ⓗ Supreme Court.
- Ⓙ Day Court.

*Hint: Look for this sentence in the passage.*

3 **What was Sandra's dream?**

***Her dream was to study law.***

*Hint: Look at sentence 9.*



GO ON



# Objective 2: Identifying Supporting Ideas

Reading Skills: Identifying facts and details, recognizing sequence of events, following directions, identifying setting

SAY: **Turn to Objective 2, Identifying Supporting Ideas, on page 13**

Check to see that all students find page 13.

SAY: **In this lesson you will practice answering questions about identifying supporting ideas. Now look at the sentence that begins with the words *facts or details.***

Read the two sentences to students.

SAY: **Now look at the first passage. Read the passage silently. Then answer the question that follows. *Only men served on the Supreme Court—* Darken the circle for the correct answer. Read the hint to help you answer the question.**

Allow students time to find and mark their answer.

SAY: **The correct answer is D, *until 200 years ago.***

Check to see that all students have filled in the correct answer space. Ask students if they have any questions.

SAY: **Now you will practice answering more questions about determining word meanings. Beginning on page 13, read each passage carefully and answer the questions that follow. Darken the circle for the correct answer, or write your answer in the space provided. Answer all the questions on pages 13 through 20. The information at the top of each page will tell you what to look for, and the hints after each question will help you determine the correct answer. When you come to the words *GO ON* at the bottom of a page, continue working on the next page. When you come to the word *STOP* at the bottom of page 20, put your pencils down. You may now begin.**

Sandra married a man she met in law school. They both got jobs as lawyers. For a while, Sandra had her own law office. Then, she and her husband had a son. Sandra decided to stay home. Sandra and her husband had two more sons.

After nine years, Sandra became a judge in Arizona. She was a judge there for seven years. Then, one of the judges from the Supreme Court left. So the Supreme Court needed another judge. The President of the United States heard about Sandra. He asked her to become a judge on the Supreme Court. She eagerly said, "Yes!"

**4 The President asked Sandra Day O'Connor to be a —**

Ⓐ student at a university.

Ⓑ lawyer in Arizona.

Ⓒ judge in an Arizona court.

● judge on the Supreme Court.

*Hint: Find the section that talks about the President.*

**5 Sandra had —**

● three sons.

Ⓖ two daughters.

Ⓗ a son and a daughter.

Ⓙ four children.

*Hint: Count the number of sons mentioned in the passage.*

**6 Sandra and her husband were both —**

Ⓐ doctors.

● lawyers.

Ⓒ teachers.

Ⓓ bankers.

*Hint: Look at sentence 2.*

**7 How long did Sandra stay home with her children?**

***9 years***

*Hint: Look at sentence 7.*



GO ON



Allow students time to find and write their answers.

Review the questions and answer choices with students. Discuss with the class why one answer is correct and the others are not correct. Also check to see that students have carefully filled in their answer spaces and have completely erased any stray marks.

# Objective 2: Identifying Supporting Ideas

**It is helpful to put events in the order they happened. This may help you to understand a passage.**

Long, long ago, the ancient Greeks served a god named Zeus. They honored Zeus by giving grand festivals. The festivals were held in a place called Olympia. During the festivals, athletes showed their strength and speed. These festivals were the first Olympic Games.

In the year 776 B.C., the 200-meter race was won by a young man named Coroebus. He is the first Olympic winner on record. The next festival took place in 772 B.C. This time the Greeks wanted to offer more to their god. So, they held new sporting events. Many people came to watch them. For the next 1,000 years, the Olympics were held every four years. They always took place in Olympia.

At first, only people with money could afford to be Olympic athletes. They had the time to train and get in shape. Some of the events were horse racing, wrestling, boxing, and running. The first Olympics lasted for five days. Prizes were given on the last day. Winning was the most important part of athletics for the ancient Greeks. The winners marched in a parade toward the Temple of Zeus. Along the way, crowds tossed flowers at them. The winners wore olive wreaths. The Greeks gave prizes to the first-place winners only. People teased the losers.

The games were stopped in A.D. 393. At that time, the Romans ruled Greece. The emperor did not like the Greek gods. So, he stopped the Olympic events. The Greek temples stood empty. Over the years, they were buried by floods and earthquakes. In 1892, a Frenchman wanted to start the Olympic Games once again. He thought that the games would bring the people of the world together in peace. In 1896, he succeeded. The first modern games were held in Athens, Greece.

1 **When did the Olympic festivals stop?**

***A.D. 393***

*Hint: Look at the last paragraph.*



GO ON

2 **When were prizes given?**

Ⓐ on the first day

Ⓑ after each event

● on the fifth day

Ⓓ every day

*Hint: Look at the section mentioning the prizes.*

3 **Which of these events happened last in the story?**

Ⓕ Coroebus won a race in Olympia.

● A Frenchman wanted to start the Olympic Games once again.

Ⓗ Games were held in Athens, Greece.

Ⓙ Prizes were only given to first-place winners.

*Hint: Look at the last paragraph.*

4 **Which of these happened first in the story?**

Ⓐ The Greeks held a festival in 772 B.C.

Ⓑ The Roman emperor stopped the games in Olympia.

● The Greeks held a festival in 776 B.C.

Ⓓ Some events were horse racing, wrestling, boxing, and running.

*Hint: Look at the beginning of the story.*

5 **When were the first modern Olympic games held?**

***1896***

*Hint: Look at the section about the modern Olympics.*



GO ON

## Objective 2: Identifying Supporting Ideas

**Written directions tell you how to do something. Every step is important.**

My friend told me to meet her at her mother's office at 3 P.M. She told me to walk to building #120 on Liberty Street and then to go in the main entrance and down the flight of stairs on the left. Then, I turn left at the bottom of the stairs and go down the hall to office #3B. She will be waiting for me inside the office.

1 **To get to my friend's mother's office, I should first —**

Ⓐ take a bus.

Ⓑ take the elevator right inside the main entrance.

Ⓒ turn right at the bottom of the stairs.

● go to #120 Liberty Street.

*Hint: Read the directions. They start with the second sentence.*

Do the lights ever go out in your neighborhood? They do in ours a lot. Sometimes they go out when it is very hot and everyone is using their air conditioners. Other times, it is during a storm. Luckily, I know what to do when the lights go out. First, I get our flashlight. Then, I go around the house turning off all the lights that were on before, as well as the television and clothes dryer. Next, I call the electric company to find out what's going on. Then I go back to reading my book—using the flashlight!

2 **What is the first thing you should do if the lights go out in your house?**

***get out a flashlight***

*Hint: Read the directions. They start with the word "first."*



GO ON

I do not like cooking. I do enjoy baking. I think that it is a lot of fun to bake a cake for a party. My favorite cake is plain yellow, because then I can put any kind of icing on it. Here is the recipe:

Step 1: Make a list of all the things you need to get at the store to make the cake.
Step 2: When you have everything, measure the right amount of water.
Step 3: Mix the water with the cake mix and two eggs.
Step 4: Bake it in the oven for about thirty minutes.
Step 5: Take the cake out of the oven and let it cool.
Step 6: Ice the cake with any flavor you like: vanilla, chocolate, or strawberry.

3 **When do you put the cake in the oven?**

Ⓕ Step 2

Ⓖ Step 3

● Step 4

Ⓙ Step 5

*Hint: Read the steps in order, starting with Step 1.*

4 **Before you start to make a cake, you should —**

Ⓐ mix the water with the eggs.

Ⓑ mix the cake mix with the eggs.

● make sure you have all the ingredients you need.

Ⓓ take the top off the can of icing you bought at the store.

*Hint: Read the steps in order, starting with Step 1.*

5 **What should you do right after you bake the cake?**

***Take the cake out of the oven and let it cool.***

*Hint: Read the steps starting with Step 4.*



GO ON

# Objective 2: Identifying Supporting Ideas

**The setting of a story lets you know when and where the story is taking place.**

Richard Byrd stood outside the small cabin on March 28, 1934. He shook hands with the men who were leaving. They were heading back to the main camp on the east coast of Antarctica. He would stay at the base camp for the winter. There was plenty of food and fuel in the tiny cabin. He felt sure nothing would go wrong.

But something did go wrong. Byrd was burning kerosene for heat, and the fumes were poisoning him. He continued to make his radio messages, because he didn't want anyone to try to rescue him in the dangerous weather. Byrd managed to stay alive until August, when three men arrived at the base camp. They hardly recognized Byrd. He was very thin and looked terrible. Byrd greeted them and then fell to the ground. The men had arrived in the nick of time. After two months of care, Byrd's good health returned.

1 **The story takes place —**

Ⓐ 100 years ago.

Ⓑ within the past 25 years.

● over 60 years ago.

Ⓓ in 1943.

*Hint: Read the first sentence.*

2 **The story takes place —**

Ⓕ at the main camp.

Ⓖ on the coast of Antarctica.

Ⓗ in a large cabin.

● at the base camp.

*Hint: Read the first paragraph.*

3 **When was Richard Byrd rescued?**

***He was rescued in August.***

*Hint: Find the section that talks about Byrd's rescue.*



GO ON

The strongest earthquake in the United States happened in Missouri. It took place in 1811. The center of the earthquake was near a town called New Madrid. Since few people lived near this town, nobody was killed. But the earthquake was quite strong. It changed the course of the Mississippi River.

**4 When did the earthquake occur?**

- Ⓐ in 1911
- Ⓑ in 1918
- ● in 1811
- Ⓓ in 1981

*Hint: Look at the second sentence.*

**5 Where was the earthquake?**

***in Missouri***

*Hint: Read the first three sentences.*

Going to the horse show on that beautiful summer day was a great experience. Before the events started, we were able to get very close to the riders and their horses. Then, after we found our seats, we spent the afternoon watching each rider and horse perform. At the end of the day, the best performers were given ribbons and prizes.

**6 When is this story taking place?**

- ● in the summer
- Ⓖ in the spring
- Ⓗ at night
- Ⓙ in the morning

*Hint: Look at the first sentence.*



STOP

## Objective 3: Summarizing Main Ideas

**The main idea is the meaning of a passage. Many times it is a sentence in the passage.**

A chameleon is a kind of lizard. Its skin is clear, but it can change color. Under its skin are layers of cells. These cells have yellow, black, and red color in them. Anger makes these colors darken. Fear makes them lighten. It also makes yellow spots appear. Temperature and light can also cause the colors to change. These changes make the chameleon hard to see. Changing colors can save a chameleon's life.

1 **What is the main idea of this story?**

***A chameleon's ability to change colors can save its life.***

*Hint: What does the whole story talk about?*



Don't worry if there are times when you get angry. Getting angry can be both good and bad. Many doctors think that it's all right to show your anger sometimes. People who get angry once in a while may live happier lives. But people must be careful when they are angry. Angry people don't always think clearly. They can do things that they may be sorry about later.

2 **What is the main idea of this story?**

- Ⓐ People can't think straight when they are angry.
- Ⓑ People get angry about nothing.
- ● Anger can be both good and bad.
- Ⓓ Anger can make you sick.

*Hint: Which choice sums up the whole passage?*

John Chapman planted apple trees in Ohio in the early 1800s. He carried the seeds all over the country. He sold the seeds or just gave them away to people. Chapman was a very kind man. He loved people, animals, and trees. The story of Johnny Appleseed is the story of his life.

3 **What is the main idea of this story?**

- Ⓕ Apple trees grow from seeds.
- ● We get the story of Johnny Appleseed from the life of John Chapman.
- Ⓗ John Chapman lived in Ohio.
- Ⓙ John Chapman traveled the country.

*Hint: What does the whole story talk about?*

GO ON



# Objective 3: Summarizing Main Ideas

Reading Skills: Identifying and summarizing the main idea

SAY: **Turn to Objective 3, Summarizing Main Ideas, on page 21.**

Check to see that all students find page 21.

SAY: **In this lesson you will practice answering questions about the main idea of a passage. Now look at the sentence that begins with the words *the main idea.***

Read the two sentences to students.

SAY: **Now look at the first passage. Read the passage silently. Then answer the question that follows. *What is the main idea of this story?* Read the hint to help you answer the question.**

Allow students time to find and write their answer.

SAY: **The main idea of the story is that *a chameleon's ability to change colors can save its life.***

Check to see that all students have written the correct answer. Ask students if they have any questions.

SAY: **Now you will practice answering more questions about summarizing the main idea. Beginning on page 21, read each passage carefully and answer the questions that follow. Darken the circle for the correct answer, or write your answer in the space provided. Answer all the questions on pages 21 through 24. The information at the top of each page will tell you what to look for, and the hints after each question will help you determine the correct answer. When you come to the words GO ON at the bottom of a page, continue working on the next page. When you come to the word STOP at the bottom of page 24, put your pencils down. You may now begin.**

Allow students time to find and write their answers.

Review the questions and answer choices with students. Discuss with the class why one answer is correct and the others are not correct. Also check to see that students have carefully filled in their answer spaces and have completely erased any stray marks.

Sometimes, people need help when they get older. Older people may need help walking or cooking food. At night, they count on their families to do these things for them. But during the day, they may be left at home alone. To help them, some cities have built day-care centers. Older people can go to these centers during the day. There they will get the help they need.

**4 What is the main idea of this story?**

- ● Older people can get the help they need in day-care centers.
- Ⓑ Older people cook their lunch.
- Ⓒ Families are busy at night.
- Ⓓ Older people need help walking.

*Hint: All of the sentences in the paragraph give you the main idea.*

A man in Florida can talk to fish. He spent a long time learning how to do this. First, he watched fish very closely. Then, he listened to the noises they made. Finally, he learned to make the same sounds. Sometimes, the fish listen to him. At times he can even make them do things. This man thinks that someday fishermen might be able to call fish to their nets.

**5 What is the main idea of this story?**

- Ⓕ Some fish listen to sounds.
- Ⓖ Many people like to fish.
- Ⓗ Fish never listen.
- ● A man in Florida talks to fish.

*Hint: What does the whole story talk about?*



GO ON

# Objective 3: Summarizing Main Ideas

**A good summary contains the main idea of a passage. It is short but includes the most important points.**

One kind of spider makes a web underwater. It weaves its web in water plants. Then, it carries bubbles of air down to fill the web. The water spider lies still on its web. Soon, a water insect swims near it. The spider dashes out and catches the insect. It brings its catch back to the air-filled web to eat.

1 **Which sentence tells what this story is mostly about?**

- Ⓐ Some spiders look better underwater.
- Ⓑ Water spiders build their webs using air bubbles.
- Ⓒ Water spiders like water insects.
- ● One kind of spider can live underwater very well.

*Hint: Which sentence tells you about the whole passage?*

It is hard to think of doctors as artists. But their job of healing people can be beautiful. For instance, doctors help people who can't hear well. In some cases, doctors use a piece of a rib. They carve the rib so that it fits inside the ear. The bone is about a tenth of an inch high. It also has a pretty and interesting shape. With this bone in the ear, the person can hear much better.

2 **What is the best summary of this passage?**

- ● Some people think that a doctor is a kind of artist because healing people is beautiful.
- Ⓖ People who can't hear well need to use their ribs to try to hear better.
- Ⓗ Artists know how to carve ribs into pretty shapes.
- Ⓙ Doctors help artists hear better using pieces of ribs.

*Hint: Which sentence tells you about the whole passage?*

Calamity Jane was a famous woman of the Wild West. She was famous because she was so tough. She lived during the 1800s. She learned to ride a horse and shoot a gun at an early age. People could always hear her coming. She also liked to dress in men's clothes. There weren't many women like her.

3 **What is this story mostly about?**

Ⓐ It was tough for Calamity Jane to live during the 1800s.

Ⓑ Calamity Jane was famous because she was taught to ride a horse.

● Calamity Jane did things that other women in the 1800s did not.

Ⓓ Calamity Jane wore men's clothes.

*Hint: Which sentence sums up Calamity Jane?*

Cats are very much like lions and tigers. They can jump high in the air. Cats can jump seven feet high. They have padded feet. That way they can sneak up on their prey. Cats have 18 claws on their feet. They can push out and draw back their claws.

4 **What is this story mostly about?**

***How cats are very much like lions and tigers.***

*Hint: Which sentence tells you about the whole passage?*

Two things make a tree a conifer. One is that it must make seeds in its cones. It must also have needle-like leaves. Conifers are called evergreen trees. They look green all the time. Conifers do lose and replace their leaves. But they never lose all their leaves at the same time.

5 **What is this story mostly about?**

***What makes a tree a conifer.***

*Hint: Which sentence tells you about the whole paragraph?*



STOP

## Objective 4: Perceiving Relationships and Recognizing Outcomes

**Knowing what happened (effect) and what made it happen (cause) helps you to understand what you read.**

The big dance was Friday night, and Jodi needed a dress to wear. As she was sorting through her closet, her older sister, Gabriela, tapped her on the shoulder. She knew that Jodi had always liked her blue dress. "How would you like to wear this?" she asked. Jodi's eyes lit up. She hugged Gabriela and ran to try on the dress.

1 **Why was Jodi happy?**

***Gabriela let Jodi borrow her blue dress.***

*Hint: Jodi's eyes lighting up is the effect. What made this happen?*

2 **Why did Jodi need a dress to wear?**

Ⓐ She wanted to be like her older sister, Gabriela.

● The big dance was Friday night.

Ⓒ She was tired of blue dresses in her closet.

Ⓓ She couldn't find any dresses in her closet.

*Hint: Jodi needing a dress is the effect. What made this happen?*

GO ON





# Objective 4: Perceiving Relationships and Recognizing Outcomes

Reading Skills: Identifying cause and effect and predicting events.

SAY: **Turn to Objective 4, Perceiving Relationships and Recognizing Outcomes, on page 25.**

Check to see that all students find page 25.

SAY: **In this lesson you will practice answering questions about cause-and-effect relationships and predicting what will happen next. Now look at the sentence that begins with the words *knowing what happened.***

Read the sentence to students.

SAY: **Now look at the first passage. Read the passage silently. Then answer the question that follows. *Why was Jodi happy?* Read the hint to help you answer the question.**

Allow students time to find and write their answer.

SAY: **Jodi was happy because Gabriela let Jodi borrow her blue dress.**

Check to see that all students have written in the correct answer.
Ask students if they have any questions.

SAY: **Now you will practice answering more questions about cause-and-effect relationships and predicting what will happen next. Beginning on page 25, read each passage carefully and answer the questions that follow. Darken the circle for the correct answer, or write your answer in the space provided. Answer all the questions on pages 25 through 28. The information at the top of each page will tell you what to look for, and the hints after each question will help you determine the correct answer. When you come to the words *GO ON* at the bottom of a page, continue working on the next page. When you come to the word *STOP* at the bottom of page 28, put your pencils down. You may now begin.**

Alex and Vince were spending a week at camp. Tonight was their last night, and it was "skit night." The campers in each cabin had written plays about their camp experiences. Alex had seen how easily Vince made friends with everyone in the camp. When Vince was chosen to be the announcer for skit night, Alex dumped a box of cookie crumbs in Vince's sleeping bag.

3 **Why did the campers write plays about their camp experiences?**

- Ⓕ They liked to write plays.
- Ⓖ They had so much fun at camp that they had a lot to write about.
- ● They were going to put on skits.
- Ⓙ Their camp counselors asked them to write plays.

*Hint: Writing plays is the effect. What made this happen?*

4 **Why did Alex dump a box of cookie crumbs in Vince's sleeping bag?**

- ● Vince was chosen to be the announcer for skit night.
- Ⓑ Alex knew how much his friend liked cookies.
- Ⓒ Alex wanted to have a party in the cabin after skit night.
- Ⓓ Vince needed more cookies because he had so many friends.

*Hint: Alex dumping a box of cookies in Vince's sleeping bag is the effect. What made this happen?*

5 **Why was Vince chosen as the announcer for skit night?**

***Vince was friends with everyone at camp.***

*Hint: Being chosen as announcer is the effect. What made this happen?*

Trena's baseball team was not very good. It had not won a game all season. Something had to be done, or else the team would be laughed at by everyone in town. So, Trena promised to eat one bug for every run the team scored. That night, the team scored twenty runs and finally won a game.

6 **Why hadn't Trena's baseball team won a game all season?**

- Ⓕ Everyone in town laughed at the team.
- Ⓖ The team ate bugs and got sick.
- ● The team was not very good.
- Ⓙ Something interrupted practices.

*Hint: Not winning a game is the effect. What made this happen?*

7 **Why did the team score twenty runs?**

- Ⓐ They ate bugs before the game.
- Ⓑ They had many fans in town.
- Ⓒ There were twenty girls on the team.
- ● Trena had promised to eat one bug for every run scored.

*Hint: Scoring twenty runs is the effect. What made this happen?*



GO ON



Allow students time to find and write their answers.

Review the questions and answer choices with students. Discuss with the class why one answer is correct and the others are not correct. Also check to see that students have carefully filled in their answer spaces and have completely erased any stray marks.

## Objective 4: Perceiving Relationships and Recognizing Outcomes

**Many times you can tell in advance what is probably going to happen next. You must think about what would make sense if the story were to go on.**

In the morning, Becky came downstairs. "I don't like this house at all," the girl told her parents. "It smells funny." Her mother asked if she had seen the wild strawberries growing in the front yard. Her father mentioned the pony he had seen at the neighboring house. The girl's eyes lit up.

1 **What will Becky probably do?**

- Ⓐ The family will sell the house and move because of the smell.
- Ⓑ The father will buy the pony for Becky.
- ● Becky will find some things she likes about that house.
- Ⓓ Becky will get angry because her eyes have lit up.

*Hint: Think about how Becky feels at the end of the story, before you make your choice.*

The man was trying to balance himself. His bicycle was picking up speed on the steep hill. He hit a bump, and one foot lost its grip on the pedal.

2 **What will probably happen next?**

***The man will fall off the bicycle.***

*Hint: Picture the scene in your mind before writing the answer.*

The shaggy animal went up to the backdoor. It rattled the screen door with its front paw and then sat down. It was quiet for a while. But soon a face appeared at the door, and then there was a scream of joy. "It's Goldie!" a girl's voice said. "She's come back."

3 **What will the girl probably do next?**

- Ⓕ run to get her mother
- ● open the door to let Goldie in
- Ⓗ shut and lock the inside door
- Ⓙ scream again

*Hint: What is most likely to happen next?*



GO ON

Valentina Tereshkova was nervous. She knew she'd soon make history. It was a still morning. She sat strapped in her seat. At last, the Soviet spaceship began to shake. Its great engines roared. The ship climbed from the launch pad. It built up speed. Soon, it was racing through the sky. Valentina had become the first woman in space.

**4 What will Valentina probably do next?**

- Ⓐ call her mother
- Ⓑ have lunch
- ● follow the steps she was trained to do in space
- Ⓓ rest so that she could think clearly

*Hint: What seems most likely to happen based on all the sentences?*

Cris looked at the window to make sure it was open. Then she marked her place and closed the book. She put it on the table next to her bed. Then she fluffed up the pillow and set the alarm clock.

**5 What will Cris most likely do next?**

- Ⓕ fall asleep
- Ⓖ have a snack
- ● get into bed
- Ⓙ take a shower

*Hint: Read the entire paragraph.*

When Sammy woke up, he looked out the window. The slopes were covered with snow. Quickly, he pulled on his long underwear and other warm clothes. He ate a good, hot breakfast so that he'd have plenty of energy. Then he checked his equipment. He walked in his heavy boots toward the door.

**6 What is probably going to happen next?**

- ● Sammy is going to ski down the slopes.
- Ⓑ Sammy is going ice skating.
- Ⓒ Sammy is going to play golf.
- Ⓓ Sammy is going to stay inside.

*Hint: You need to read the whole paragraph, but especially the last sentence.*



STOP

## Objective 5: Making Inferences and Generalizations

**The way a character acts tells you about that person's mood.**

Al had been standing in line at the counter waiting to pay for the things he had chosen. The store was hot, and the air conditioning didn't work. Al was holding some heavy objects, and he wished the line would move faster. A woman cut to the front of the line. People protested, but the woman didn't budge. Suddenly, Al threw his things into a nearby cart and walked quickly out of the store.

1 **How was Al feeling when he left the store?**

Ⓐ Al had gotten tired of waiting and planned to come back when the store wasn't so busy.

Ⓑ Al was hungry and looking forward to lunch.

● Al was angry that he had waited so long only to have someone cut into the line.

Ⓓ Al felt that he had chosen the wrong items.

*Hint: Carefully think about the entire passage, especially the last sentence.*

Ian and Louise were supposed to be planting corn, beans, and carrots together. While Louise dug up the old garden and turned over the soil, Ian sat under a tree sipping a cool drink. While Louise dug in fertilizer and raked the garden, Ian ate his lunch. When the soil was finally ready for the seeds to be planted, Ian said to Louise, "I'll plant the seeds." Louise yelled back, "No, thanks! I'll plant the seeds!"

2 **How did Louise feel?**

***angry because she has to do all the work***

*Hint: You must read the entire passage and what Louise said at the end of the story to find out how Louise felt.*



GO ON



# Objective 5: Making Inferences and Generalizations

Reading Skills: Interpreting graphs and diagrams, inferring information, making generalizations and judgments, and drawing conclusions

SAY: **Turn to Objective 5, Making Inferences and Generalizations, on page 29.**

Check to see that all students find page 29.

SAY: **In this lesson you will practice answering questions about graphs and diagrams, making judgments, and reaching conclusions. Now look at the sentence that begins with the words *the way a character acts.***

Read the sentence to students.

SAY: **Now look at the first passage. Read the passage silently. Then answer the question that follows. *How was Al feeling when he left the store?* Darken the circle for the correct answer. Read the hint to help you answer the question.**

Allow students time to find and mark their answer.

SAY: **The correct answer is C, *Al was angry that he had waited so long only to have someone cut into the line.***

Check to see that all students have filled in the correct answer space. Ask students if they have any questions.

SAY: **Now you will practice answering more questions about graphs and diagrams, making judgments, and reaching conclusions. Beginning on page 29, read each passage carefully and answer the questions that follow. Darken the circle for the correct answer, or write your answer in the space provided. Answer all the questions on pages 29 and 30. The information at the top of each page will tell you what to look for, and the hints after each question will help you determine the correct answer. When you come to the words *GO ON* at the bottom of a page, continue working on the next page. When you come to the word *STOP* at the bottom of page 30, put your pencils down. You may now begin.**

Allow students time to find and write their answers.

When the baby came home from the hospital, his five-year-old brother, Mike, shouted, "Take it back! You got a new baby because I'm not good enough for you!" Mike's parents talked with him for a long time. They told him that the baby would need special care at first. But that didn't mean they didn't love Mike anymore.

3 **How did Mike feel about his new baby brother?**

- Ⓕ Mike was mad because the baby cried all the time.
- Ⓖ Mike was mad because he didn't want to take care of the baby.
- ● Mike felt his parents loved the new baby more than they loved him.
- Ⓙ Mike felt that the baby should not get special care.

*Hint: Read what Mike said to discover how he felt.*

A fisherman brought a large fish to the king and was paid well for it. As the fisherman left, he picked up a valuable coin off the floor. The angry king called to him, "That is not yours." The man answered, "I did not want someone to step on the king's face. That is why I picked up the coin." The king smiled and let the man keep the coin.

4 **How did the king feel after the man said something?**

***He was happy because the man did not want to keep the coin.***

*Hint: Carefully think about the entire passage, especially what the king did at the end of the passage.*



STOP



Review the questions and answer choices with students. Discuss with the class why one answer is correct and the others are not correct. Also check to see that students have carefully filled in their answer spaces and have completely erased any stray marks.

## Objective 6: Recognizing Points of View, Facts, and Opinions

**It is important to know the difference between fact and opinion. A fact is real and true. An opinion is a feeling or belief. Words that describe are used to offer opinions.**

Stephen Hawking is a famous scientist. He has written books about physics and our universe. But Hawking must do all his work in a wheelchair. In his twenties, he found out that he had Lou Gehrig's disease. Later, he lost his power to speak and write. Now, he does all his work on a special computer. The computer allows him to speak.

1 **Why does Stephen Hawking use a computer?**

***The computer helps him speak.***

*Hint: A fact is real and true. What is said in the passage?*

A sundog is a bright ring around the sun. Sometimes, the sundog will also have colors. It may look like a round rainbow. Sundogs are caused by ice crystals high in the sky. You should never look right at the sun. So wear sunglasses if you want to see a sundog.

2 **Which of these is an OPINION from the passage?**

- Ⓐ A sundog is caused by ice crystals.
- Ⓑ You should not look right at the sun.
- ● The rainbow colors of a sundog are beautiful.
- Ⓓ A sundog is a bright ring around the sun.

*Hint: Words that describe are opinion words.*



GO ON



# Objective 6: Recognizing Points of View, Facts, and Opinions

Reading Skills: Recognizing the author's point of view and distinguishing between fact and opinion

SAY: **Turn to Objective 6, Recognizing Points of View, Facts, and Opinions, on page 31.**

Check to see that all students find page 31.

**SAY: In this lesson you will practice answering questions about recognizing the author's point of view. Now look at the sentence that begins with the words *it is important to know.***

Read the four sentences to students.

**SAY: Now look at the first passage. Read the passage silently. Then answer the question that follows. *Why does Stephen Hawking use a computer?* Darken the circle for the correct answer. Read the hint to help you answer the question.**

Allow students time to find and write their answer.

**SAY: *Stephen Hawking uses a computer to help him speak.***

Check to see that all students have written the correct answer.
Ask students if they have any questions.

SAY: **Now you will practice answering more questions about recognizing the author's point of view, and distinguishing between fact and opinion. Beginning on page 31, read each passage carefully and answer the questions that follow. Darken the circle for the correct answer, or write your answer in the space provided. Answer all the questions on pages 31 and 32. The information at the top of each page will tell you what to look for, and the hints after each question will help you determine the correct answer. When you come to the words *GO ON* at the bottom of a page, continue working on the next page. When you come to the word *STOP* at the bottom of page 32, put your pencils down. You may now begin.**

Allow students time to find and write their answers.

Did you know that your body shrinks as the day goes by? When you wake up, you are at your tallest. Your body is relaxed. Your muscles are stretched, and your joints are loose. As the day passes, your muscles tighten. Gravity pulls down on your body, too. Your body may be an inch shorter by the end of the day.

3 **Which of these is a FACT from the passage?**

- Ⓕ When you wake up, you feel good because your body is relaxed.
- Ⓖ It is good that your muscles tighten so that you don't fall down.
- ● Gravity pulls down on your body.
- Ⓙ It's better to be short than tall.

*Hint: Words like "feel good," "it is good," and "it is better" are opinion words.*

Have you ever watched a pond freeze in winter? The water freezes first on the top. The ice forms a very thin sheet across the water. It takes only about twenty minutes for this sheet to form. Then slowly the ice begins to grow down toward the bottom. It takes an hour for the first sheet to become two times as thick as it was when it started.

4 **Which of these is NOT a fact from the passage?**

- ● When ice freezes it looks pretty.
- Ⓑ It takes about twenty minutes for the first sheet of ice to form.
- Ⓒ It takes an hour for the first sheet to become two times as thick.
- Ⓓ Ice freezes first on top, forming a very thin sheet across the water.

*Hint: Facts are real and true. Which sentence is an opinion?*

For years, traveling farm workers were not treated well. At last, Cesar Chavez could stand it no longer. He thought farm workers should be paid more. He wanted better working conditions for them. To gain these, he formed a union. The group went on strike to get what they wanted.

5 **Which of these is a FACT from the passage?**

- Ⓕ It was not fair that farm workers were not treated well.
- Ⓖ Better working conditions mean that farm workers will produce more.
- ● To gain better working conditions, Cesar Chavez formed a union.
- Ⓙ It is not a good idea to go on strike.

*Hint: A fact is real and true. What is actually said in the passage?*



STOP



Review the questions and answer choices with students. Discuss with the class why one answer is correct and the others are not correct. Also check to see that students have carefully filled in their answer spaces and have completely erased any stray marks.

UNIT THREE

# Reading Comprehension

**Directions: Read each story carefully. Then read each question. Darken the circle for the correct answer, or write in the answer.**

**TRY THIS** — **More than one answer choice may seem correct. Choose the answer that goes best with the story.**

**Sample A** **Our Pancakes**

Dad and I made our own breakfast. We made pancakes. They tasted better than Mom's pancakes. Dad and I decided we would keep this as our little secret.

**Why will they keep the secret?**

- Ⓐ They do not want Mom to know they cooked breakfast.
- ● They do not want to hurt Mom's feelings.
- Ⓒ They burned the pancakes.
- Ⓓ They want to make breakfast again next week.

**THINK IT THROUGH** — **The correct answer is B, They do not want to hurt Mom's feelings. The story states that the pancakes tasted better than Mom's pancakes, but they will keep this secret rather than hurt Mom's feelings.**

STOP

## Jill and Jo

Jill and Jo were playing. Jo ran to hide. Jill looked for her. Then it began to rain. Jill and Jo got wet. They ran to the house.

1 **What were the girls playing?**

*hide-and-seek*

2 **Why did Jill and Jo run to the house?**

- Ⓐ because they were tired
- Ⓑ because it was hot
- ● because it was raining
- Ⓓ because it was time for lunch

GO ON





# Unit 3: Reading Comprehension

## Reading Selections

Reading Skills: Understanding explicitly stated details, actions, reasons, sequence of events; making inferences; inferring meaning; extending meaning; making predictions; understanding implicit ideas; identifying author's purpose

SAY: **Turn to Reading Selections on page 33.**

Check to see that all students find page 33.

SAY: **On page 33 you will practice answering questions about stories that you read.**

Read the Directions to students.

SAY: **Now look at Try This.**

**Read Try This to students.**

SAY: **Now look at Sample A. Read the story silently. Then answer the question that follows. Why will they keep the secret? Darken the circle for the correct answer.**

Allow students time to find and mark their answer. Remind students to carefully fill in the answer space and to completely erase any stray marks.

SAY: **Now look at Think It Through.**

Read Think It Through to students. Check to see that all students have filled in the correct answer space. Ask students if they have any questions.

SAY: **Now you will practice answering more questions about stories that you read. Beginning on page 33, read each selection carefully and answer the questions that follow. Do numbers 1 through 30 just as we did Sample A. Darken the circle for the correct answer. When you come to the arrow with the words *GO ON* at the bottom of a page, continue working on the next page. When you come to the stop sign at the bottom of page 40, put your pencils down. You may now begin.**

Allow students time to find and mark their answers.

## The Girls Get Lost!

Sheila used to live in a large city where she had many friends. When her mother got a job in a small town, Sheila was upset. She didn't want to move. She didn't want to leave her friends, especially her best friend, Katie. Sheila's mother promised that they would arrange a visit with Katie soon.

One day Sheila's mother asked her, "How would you like to go to the zoo on Saturday? I just talked to Mrs. Lee on the phone. She and Katie can meet us there." Sheila was excited. She couldn't think of anything she'd rather do.

The next Saturday was cold and clear. Sheila put on many layers of warm clothing. She had made a book for Katie. It told all about the fun things they had done when they lived next door to each other.

When Sheila and her mother drove up to the zoo, they saw Katie and her mother waiting at the entrance. Sheila and Katie were glad to see each other. They hurried down the path to the monkey house. "Wait for us there," Mrs. Lee said. But the girls were so busy talking that they didn't even hear her.

The girls watched the gorillas for a while. They had never seen such large apes. Then they ran to the area with lions and tigers.

They bought some food for the elephants and fed them. They spent a long time watching a giraffe and its baby.

When they started getting hungry, they turned around to look for their mothers, but they couldn't find them anywhere. "Uh oh! I think we might be in trouble," Sheila said. Katie was worried, too. The girls sat down and tried to think of what to do.

They decided to follow the signs back to the entrance.

When they had walked a long time, they saw their mothers. Their mothers were happy to see them. They had been worried about the girls. "Where have you been? We've been looking everywhere for you!" Sheila's mother said. The girls didn't know what to say. Later Katie whispered to Sheila. "Well, I guess we can add another chapter to the book you wrote. We can write about the time we got lost at the zoo."



GO ON

3 **The boxes below show events that happened in the story.**

| 1 | 2 | 3 |
|---|---|---|
| **The girls met at the zoo.** | | **The girls fed the elephants.** |

**What belongs in the second box?**

Ⓕ The girls watched a giraffe.

Ⓖ The girls started getting hungry.

● The girls watched the gorillas.

Ⓙ The girls found their mothers.

4 **Which question does the first paragraph answer?**

● Why was Sheila upset?

Ⓑ What is the name of the small town where Sheila moved?

Ⓒ How did the girls get lost?

Ⓓ What is Katie's favorite food?

5 **Why were the mothers upset?**

***they were worried***

6 **What is this story mainly about?**

Ⓕ Sheila's move to a small town

Ⓖ Sheila's mother's new job

Ⓗ the monkey house

● the girls' day at the zoo

7 **Why did Mrs. Lee tell the girls to wait for their mothers at the monkey house?**

Ⓐ She liked monkeys.

● She did not want the girls to get lost.

Ⓒ She was cold.

Ⓓ She was talking to Sheila's mother.

8 **What was the weather like on the day the girls visited the zoo?**

Ⓕ hot

Ⓖ cold and cloudy

Ⓗ rainy

● cold and clear

9 **A gorilla is a—**

Ⓐ type of lion.

Ⓑ type of fish.

Ⓒ kind of elephant.

● large ape.

GO ON

## Making a Clay Pot

With practice, anyone can make a simple pot from clay. Take a piece of clay the size of an apple and put it on a flat surface. Press and squeeze it until there are no lumps or air bubbles. Then, using both hands, shape the clay into a smooth, round ball.

Now you are ready to begin. Keep the ball in your left hand. With the thumb of your right hand, make an opening in the clay. Press down toward your palm, leaving a half inch of clay at the bottom. This will be the base of your pot. Now keep your thumb inside the pot. Press the clay gently between your thumb and fingers. Turn the pot after each squeeze. This will make the pot thin out evenly. Continue squeezing and turning until the pot it as thin as you want it.

Now the pot must dry. Cover it with plastic so that it won't dry too quickly. After a few days, uncover it. Then wait a few more days. When the pot is completely dry, it is ready to be fired in a special oven called a kiln. After the firing, the pot will keep its shape.

You may want to add color to your pot. In this case, you would put a glaze on the pot and fire it in the kiln a second time.

**10 Why is the pot covered with plastic?**

*to keep moisture in the pot for a while*

**11 In this story, you can tell that a kiln is a—**

- Ⓕ cover for the pot.
- Ⓖ glaze for the pot.
- ● special oven to bake the pot.
- Ⓙ special case to store the pot.

**12 The first thing you should do when making a pot is to—**

- ● press and squeeze out all the lumps and air bubbles from the clay.
- Ⓑ cover the clay with plastic.
- Ⓒ shape the clay into a ball.
- Ⓓ make the base of the pot.

**13 Why should you turn the pot after each squeeze?**

- Ⓕ so the pot will keep its shape
- Ⓖ so the pot will have a base
- ● so the pot won't be too thick in some spots
- Ⓙ to remove your thumb



GO ON

## An Invitation

### Holiday Fun!

All members of the Boys and Girls Club of Smithtown are invited to a Fourth of July party on July 4, 1998. The party will be held at the home of club sponsors Frank and Marie Brown.

The party will start at 6:30 P.M. Hamburgers, potato salad, watermelon, and other goodies will be served. Bring your turtle for the annual turtle race. At dark, fireworks will be viewed from the balcony. Sparklers and noisemakers will be provided. A marshmallow roast will be held following the fireworks.

It should be a lot of fun. See you on the 4th!

**14 When will the party take place?**

*July 4, 1998*

**15 What should the guests bring?**

● a turtle
Ⓑ watermelon
Ⓒ a swimsuit
Ⓓ potato salad

**16 According to the invitation, after the fireworks, the guests will—**

Ⓕ eat ice cream.
Ⓖ race turtles.
● roast marshmallows.
Ⓙ eat dinner.

**17 What time will the party start?**

● 6:30 P.M.
Ⓑ 2:00 P.M.
Ⓒ 10:00 A.M.
Ⓓ You cannot tell from the invitation.



GO ON

## Learning About Apples

People have been eating apples for a very long time. When the first pioneers came to America, there were only small, sour apples called crab apples. These apples were not good to eat. Later, pioneers brought apple seeds from their homes in Europe.

In 1625 a man in Boston planted the first apple orchard in America. After that, when a pioneer family picked a place to live, one of the first things they did was choose an area and plant apple seeds. Soon, there were many apple trees in America.

The pioneers used apples in many ways. They made apple juice, apple butter, and apple pie. Sometimes they used apples as food for their animals.

Today we have refrigerators and grocery stores. We have fresh fruits and vegetables even in the winter. They are trucked in from warm places and sold in our stores. But the pioneers had no trucks or stores. They had no fresh fruits and vegetables during the long winters.

The pioneers soon learned how to preserve fruits and vegetables. They found that if fruit was dried, it would last and would not spoil. They could make apples last through the winter.

In the fall they picked the apples. Then many families would meet for a work party. They would talk and work at the same time. They peeled the apples and cut out the cores. Then they sliced the apples and laid them on a big net. About a week later, the apples were dried. They would keep for many months. The apples could be eaten dried, or they could be soaked in water and made into pies.

GO ON

**18 What does the word orchard mean?**

Ⓕ a type of apple

Ⓖ a pioneer

● a group of fruit trees

Ⓙ a type of store

**19 Why did the pioneers have work parties to dry the apples?**

Ⓐ to make them dry faster

● to visit and work at the same time

Ⓒ to earn money

Ⓓ to find new jobs

**20 Why were apple seeds brought to America by the pioneers?**

***to plant for food***

**21 This story was probably written to tell—**

Ⓕ about pioneer work parties.

Ⓖ about the first apple orchard in America.

Ⓗ how to preserve apples.

● about the history of the apple in America.

**22 In order to answer question 21, the reader should—**

● look for the word preserve in the story.

Ⓑ reread the last word in each paragraph.

Ⓒ read other stories about apples.

Ⓓ reread the first sentence in each paragraph.

**23 The pioneers used apples in all the following ways except as—**

Ⓕ food for animals.

Ⓖ juice.

Ⓗ butter.

● a glue.

**24 You would probably find this story in a book called—**

● *A History of America's Favorite Foods.*

Ⓑ *Orchard Do's and Don'ts.*

Ⓒ *Famous Early Americans.*

Ⓓ *How to Preserve Fruits.*

**25 In this story, the word preserve means—**

● to keep from spoiling.

Ⓖ to eat quickly.

Ⓗ to put in a freezer.

Ⓙ to bury in a trunk in the sand.

**26 If the story continued, it would probably be about—**

● other uses for apples.

Ⓑ how to build a barn.

Ⓒ the differences between apples and oranges.

Ⓓ pioneers in New York.



GO ON

## A Lifelong Love

When Jane Goodall was a young girl, she liked to watch animals. She learned many things about animals by watching them eat, sleep, and play. When she was older, Jane went to Africa to study wild chimpanzees. She had to live in the jungle to be near the chimpanzees all of the time. It was hard for Jane at first. The chimpanzees ran whenever she came near. Soon they were more comfortable when she was around. They let her watch them. She learned how they collected vines and made them into beds in the tops of trees. She found that they greeted each other with noises and hugs. Jane also found that the chimpanzees used tools. They poked grass into the dirt to find bugs to eat.

27 **What tool did the chimpanzees use?**

- Ⓕ dirt
- Ⓖ bugs
- Ⓗ vines
- ● grass

28 **Why did the chimpanzees collect vines?**

***make beds***

29 **Why did the chimpanzees run from Jane at first?**

- ● They were scared of her.
- Ⓑ They were playing hide-and-seek.
- Ⓒ They were racing each other.
- Ⓓ They were looking for food.

30 **This story is mainly about—**

- Ⓕ wild chimpanzees and how they live.
- ● Jane Goodall's study of wild chimpanzees.
- Ⓗ foods that chimpanzees eat.
- Ⓙ Jane Goodall's life.



STOP



Review the questions and answer choices with students. Discuss with the class why one answer is correct and the others are not correct. Also check to see that students have carefully filled in the answer spaces and have completely erased any stray marks.

## Test

Directions: Read each story carefully. Then read each question. Darken the circle for the correct answer, or write in the answer.

**TRY THIS** More than one answer choice may sound correct. Choose the answer that goes best with the story.

Sample A **Kangaroos**

Kangaroos come in all sizes. The smallest kangaroo is the musky rat. It is about six inches tall. The largest kangaroo is the red kangaroo. It is about six feet tall. It lives in the dry central part of Australia. Red kangaroos are great jumpers.

**How tall is a musky rat?**

Ⓐ about six feet

Ⓑ about six centimeters

● about six inches

Ⓓ very tiny

**THINK IT THROUGH** The correct answer is C, about six inches. The third sentence in the story contain this information.

STOP

### The Great Sphinx

The Egyptians made statues of sphinxes to honor kings or queens. A sphinx has the head of a human and the body of a lion. The oldest and largest sphinx is the Great Sphinx. It was built in the desert near Giza, Egypt, thousands of years ago. It is 240 feet long and 66 feet high. At times the Great Sphinx has been buried by sand. Weather has worn away part of the stone. Today scientists are working on ways to save the Great Sphinx. They hope special chemicals will keep it from crumbling.

1 **Why was the Great Sphinx built?**

● to honor a king or queen

Ⓑ to honor lions

Ⓒ to protect Giza, Egypt

Ⓓ to attract tourists

2 **How do scientists plan to save the Great Sphinx?**

***by using special chemicals to keep it from crumbling***

GO ON





## Test

SAY: **Turn to the Test on page 41.**

Check to see that all students find the Test.

SAY: **In this test you use the reading skills that we have practiced in this unit. Look at Sample A. Read the story silently. Then answer the question that follows. How tall is a musky rat? Darken the circle for the correct answer.**

Allow students time to find and mark their answer.

SAY: **You should have darkened the circle for *C, about six inches,* because the selection says that the musky rat is about six inches tall.**

Check to see that all students have filled in the correct answer space. Ask students if they have any questions.

SAY: **Now you will finish the test on your own. Carefully read each selection and the questions that follow. Do numbers 1 through 28 just as we did Sample A. When you come to the arrow with the words *GO ON* at the bottom of a page, continue working on the next page. When you come to the stop sign at the bottom of page 47, put your pencils down. You may now begin.**

Allow students time to find and mark their answers.

## Going to the Store

One day Mrs. Rodriguez was cooking dinner. She called her son Gabriel into the kitchen. "Please ride your bike to the store, and buy a dozen eggs," she said. She gave Gabriel two dollar bills.

On the way to the store, Gabriel passed his friend Eduardo's house. Gabriel stopped to talk for a few minutes. Then he left for the store.

At the store he found the eggs. But when he reached in his pocket, there was no money. The money had fallen out of his pocket. Gabriel got on his bike and retraced his path. He kept his eyes on the street the entire time.

When Gabriel rode up to Eduardo's house, Eduardo came running toward him. "Hey, look what I found!" he said, waving two dollars. "Let's go to the store and buy some ice cream!"

Gabriel grinned. "That's the money I just lost," he said. "I have to buy eggs with it." Eduardo looked disappointed, but he handed the money to Gabriel. "Why don't you ride your bike to the store with me?" Gabriel asked. The two boys raced down the street. They reached the store quickly. Gabriel bought the eggs. But he had forgotten to bring his backpack for carrying them. He decided the safest thing to do was to zip the eggs inside his jacket.

He had just zipped his jacket when Eduardo called out, "Race you to the corner!" Gabriel stood up to get extra speed. But his jacket was not tight enough to hold the eggs. The carton crashed to the street. Gabriel stopped and opened it. "Wow, I sure hope Mom doesn't need more than three eggs," he said to himself.

GO ON

3 **What is this story mainly about?**

Ⓕ what happened to Eduardo after school

Ⓖ what Mrs. Rodriguez prepared for dinner

Ⓗ what Gabriel ate for supper

● what happened to Gabriel on the way to the store

4 **What will probably happen next?**

Ⓐ Mrs. Rodriguez will be happy to see Gabriel.

Ⓑ Mrs. Rodriguez will reward Gabriel.

● Mrs. Rodriguez will be unhappy with Gabriel.

Ⓓ Eduardo will return to the store.

5 **How many eggs were left unbroken?**

Ⓕ none

● three

Ⓗ five

Ⓙ ten

6 **What did Eduardo want to do with the two dollars?**

● buy ice cream

Ⓑ save it

Ⓒ give it away

Ⓓ buy a game

7 **Mrs. Rodriguez sent Gabriel to the store—**

Ⓕ to return empty pop bottles.

Ⓖ to pay a bill.

● to buy eggs.

Ⓙ to meet his father.

8 **What caused the eggs to break?**

***They fell out of Gabriel's jacket.***

9 **Eduardo rode to the store with Gabriel—**

Ⓐ after dinner.

● the second time Gabriel went to the store.

Ⓒ after lunch.

Ⓓ the first time Gabriel went to the store.

10 **In this story, the word retraced means—**

● went back over the same path.

Ⓖ cooked again.

Ⓗ jumped again.

Ⓙ laughed again.



GO ON

## Spaghetti with Meat Sauce

Here's a recipe that is a favorite with many families.

You will need:

1 pound hamburger

2 cans tomato sauce

$\frac{1}{4}$ cup oil

$\frac{1}{2}$ onion, chopped

2 cloves garlic, minced

$\frac{1}{2}$ teaspoon basil

$\frac{1}{2}$ teaspoon oregano

1 package of spaghetti

In a large pan, heat the oil and brown the onions and garlic. Add the hamburger. Stir over a medium heat until the meat is browned. Add the tomato sauce, basil, and oregano. Simmer the sauce over a low heat for 25 to 30 minutes. While the sauce is simmering, boil water in a large pot. Add the spaghetti, and cook for 7 to 10 minutes. Stir frequently. Drain the spaghetti. Serve hot spaghetti with the sauce. Enjoy a terrific meal!

**11 How should you prepare the onion for cooking?**

***chop it***

**12 Why is the sauce made before cooking the spaghetti?**

Ⓐ The sauce is served first.

● The sauce needs time to cook.

Ⓒ It takes more time to cook the spaghetti.

Ⓓ Most people like the sauce better.

**13 When making spaghetti with meat sauce, the first step is to—**

Ⓕ boil water.

Ⓖ cook the hamburger.

Ⓗ add the tomato sauce.

● heat the oil.

**14 This recipe tells you to do all the following except—**

Ⓐ add basil and oregano.

● add sliced mushrooms.

Ⓒ add chopped onions.

Ⓓ add two cans of tomato sauce.



GO ON

## A Great Woman

Mae C. Jemison grew up in Chicago, Illinois. Even as a young girl she dreamed of one day becoming an astronaut. She worked hard in school and earned excellent grades.

Mae's extraordinary efforts in grade school and high school gave her the opportunity to go to Stanford University in California. It was there that she received a degree in engineering. Next, Mae enrolled in Cornell University Medical College in New York City. She received a medical degree at this college.

Her dream of becoming an astronaut came true in 1987, when she was accepted in the astronaut program. In 1992, when Jemison was 35 years old, she became the first African American female astronaut to go into space. She was aboard the space shuttle *Endeavor* along with six other astronauts. The mission of the crew members of the *Endeavor* was to test the effects of weightlessness on certain animals such as frogs and fish.

**15 What question does the last paragraph answer?**

- Ⓕ How does weightlessness affect certain animals?
- Ⓖ What makes up the astronaut training program?
- ● How did Mae C. Jemison's dream come true?
- Ⓙ Where is Stanford University?

**16 What was the mission of the space shuttle *Endeavor*?**

- Ⓐ to take pictures of Earth from space
- ● to test the effect of weightlessness on animals
- Ⓒ to launch a satellite into space
- Ⓓ to orbit Earth longer than anyone had ever done it before

**17 What was Mae C. Jemison's lifelong dream?**

***to become an astronaut***

**18 The author probably wrote this story—**

- Ⓕ to describe the mission of the space shuttle *Endeavor*.
- ● to describe the career of Mae C. Jemison.
- Ⓗ to describe the childhood of Mae C. Jemison.
- Ⓙ to explain the astronaut-training program.

GO ON

## Helping Each Other

Once an ant was crawling lazily down a country path. As the path curved near a stream, the ant realized he was thirsty. The rushing water looked so cool and clear that the ant could hardly wait to take a sip. Suddenly a gust of wind blew the poor ant right into the stream.

"Help! Someone, help! I cannot swim!" he yelled.

Up in a tree not far away, a dove heard the ant's cry for help. She reached up and with her bill plucked a small branch off the tree. In a flash she flew down to where the ant was struggling to stay above water. Carefully she lowered the branch to the water's surface near the ant.

"If you can climb onto the branch, I will carry you to safety," cooed the dove.

The ant gratefully climbed onto the branch. Then the dove lifted the branch from the water and placed it safely on the grassy bank. The ant shook water from his eyes, took a few deep breaths, and looked around to thank the dove. But the dove had flown to the top of a nearby tree.

With a wave of thanks toward the dove, the ant started back down the path. He had only gone a short distance when he noticed a hunter aiming a rifle at the helpful dove.

"This will not do!" exclaimed the ant. He hurried as fast as he could toward the hunter. The angry ant climbed with great purpose over the hunter's large brown shoe and made his way under the hunter's pants leg. Just in the nick of time, the ant took a healthy bite from the hunter's ankle. The hunter let out a loud howl of pain. The noise startled the dove, and she flew from her treetop perch to safety.

GO ON

19 **What did the dove use to save the ant?**

Ⓐ a boat
● a branch
Ⓒ her wing
Ⓓ a leaf

20 **What caused the dove to fly to safety?**

Ⓕ a rifle shot
Ⓖ the ant's scream
● the hunter's howl
Ⓙ a snapping branch

21 **According to the story, the ant got a drink of water from a—**

Ⓐ puddle of water in the road.
Ⓑ drop of rain on a leaf.
Ⓒ leaf.
● stream.

22 **Who heard the ant's cry for help?**

● a dove
Ⓖ the hunter
Ⓗ a fish
Ⓙ a butterfly

23 **What most likely would have happened if the ant had not bitten the hunter?**

Ⓐ The hunter would have stepped on the ant.
● The dove would have been shot.
Ⓒ The hunter would have fallen into the stream.
Ⓓ The dove would have gone with the ant.

24 **Why did the ant fall into the water?**

***A gust of wind blew him into the water.***

25 **You can tell this story is make-believe because—**

Ⓕ it has a hunter in it.
● animals talk in it.
Ⓗ an ant climbs onto a branch.
Ⓙ a dove flies to a treetop.

26 **What lesson can be learned from this story?**

Ⓐ Don't bite the hand that feeds you.
Ⓑ A stitch in time saves nine.
Ⓒ Slow and steady wins the race.
● One good turn deserves another.

27 **This story was probably written to—**

Ⓕ teach the reader about ants.
Ⓖ show how ants can survive in water.
Ⓗ discourage people from hunting.
● teach a lesson about helping others.

28 **You would most likely find this story in a book called—**

Ⓐ *Country Days.*
Ⓑ *Real-Life Animal Friends.*
● *Learning from Animal Tales.*
Ⓓ *How to Hunt.*

STOP





SAY: **It is now time to stop. You have completed the Test. Make sure that you have carefully filled in your answer spaces and have completely erased any stray marks. Then put your pencils down.**

After the test has been scored, review the questions and answer choices with students. If students are having difficulty with any lesson, provide them with additional practice.

UNIT FOUR

# Reading Vocabulary

## Understanding Word Meanings

**Directions: Darken the circle for the word or words that have the same or almost the same meaning as the underlined word, or write in the answer.**

**TRY THIS** Choose your answer carefully. The other choices may seem correct. Be sure to think about the meaning of the underlined word.

Sample A

A check is a kind of—

- Ⓐ box
- Ⓑ picture
- Ⓒ dance
- ● mark

**THINK IT THROUGH** The correct answer is D, mark. A check is a kind of mark. A check is not a box, a picture, or a dance.

STOP

1 Slender means—

- Ⓐ quick
- Ⓑ shy
- ● thin
- Ⓓ lost

2 What is an ache?

*pain*

3 A cap is a kind of—

- Ⓕ lock
- ● hat
- Ⓗ head
- Ⓙ coat

4 To connect is to—

- Ⓐ hit
- Ⓑ shut
- ● join
- Ⓓ belong

5 Savage means—

- Ⓕ hungry
- ● wild
- Ⓗ comfortable
- Ⓙ large

6 To oppose something is to—

- Ⓐ cheer for it
- ● be against it
- Ⓒ leave it
- Ⓓ want it

STOP





# Unit 4: Reading Vocabulary

## Understanding Word Meanings

Reading Skill: Identifying synonyms

SAY: **Turn to Understanding Word Meanings on page 48.**

Check to see that all students find page 48.

SAY: **On page 48 you will practice matching words that have similar meanings.**

Read the Directions to students.

SAY: **Now look at Try This.**

Read Try This to students.

SAY: **Now look at Sample A. Read the sentence and the answer choices carefully. *A check is a kind of—box ... picture ... dance ...mark.* Darken the circle for the word that has the same or almost the same meaning as the underlined word, *check.***

Allow students time to find and mark their answer.

SAY: **Now look at Think It Through.**

Read Think It Through to students. Check to see that all students have filled in the correct answer space. Ask students if they have any questions.

SAY: **Now you will practice matching more words that have similar meanings. Do numbers 1 through 6 just as we did Sample A. When you come to the stop sign at the bottom of page 48, put your pencils down. You may now begin.**

Allow students time to find and mark their answers.

Review the questions and answer choices with students. Discuss with the class why one answer is correct and the others are not correct. Also check to see that students have carefully filled in the answer spaces and have completely erased any stray marks.

## Matching Words with More Than One Meaning

**Directions: Darken the circle for the sentence in which the underlined word means the same as it does in the sentence in the box.**

**TRY THIS**

**Read the sentence in the box carefully. Decide what the underlined word means. Then look for the sentence in which the underlined word has the same meaning.**

Sample A

**A wave swept over the beach.**

**In which sentence does wave have the same meaning as it does in the sentence above?**

- Ⓐ We saw the flag wave in the wind.
- Ⓑ Her hair has a natural wave.
- Ⓒ I saw the pilot wave to me.
- ● The fish jumped above the wave.

**THINK IT THROUGH**

**The correct answer is D. In the sentence, The fish jumped above the wave, wave means the same as it does in the sentence in the box. A wave is "a wall of water."**

STOP

1 **She wore a circle of flowers in her hair.**

**In which sentence does circle have the same meaning as it does in the sentence above?**

- Ⓐ The plane will circle the field.
- ● Draw a circle on the paper.
- Ⓒ Cara belongs to a sewing circle.
- Ⓓ Circle your answers.

2 **Let's go out and play.**

**In which sentence does play have the same meaning as it does in the sentence above?**

- Ⓕ The band will play a new song.
- Ⓖ My team will play our first game today.
- Ⓗ My sister wrote a play.
- ● Please come to my house to play.

3 **That boy lives on our block.**

**In which sentence does block have the same meaning as it does in the sentence above?**

- Ⓐ Use this board to block the hole.
- Ⓑ The baby dropped the toy block.
- ● We drove around the block.
- Ⓓ She carved that block of marble.

4 **May I borrow some string?**

**In which sentence does string have the same meaning as it does in the sentence above?**

- Ⓕ He helped me string the lights.
- Ⓖ I bought a string of pearls.
- ● Cut the string on this package.
- Ⓙ My guitar string is broken.

STOP





# Matching Words with More Than One Meaning

Reading Skill: Using sentence context to determine word meaning of multiple-meaning words

SAY: **Turn to Matching Words with More Than One Meaning on page 49.**

Check to see that all students find page 49.

SAY: **On page 49 you will practice matching words that have more than one meaning.**

Read the Directions to students.

SAY: **Now look at Try This.**

Read Try This to students.

SAY: **Now look at Sample A. Read the sentence in the box and the question below it. A *wave* swept over the beach. In which sentence does *wave* have the same meaning as it does in the sentence above? *We saw the flag wave in the wind ... Her hair has a natural wave ... I saw the pilot wave to me ... The fish jumped above the wave.* Darken the circle for the sentence that uses the word *wave* in the same way as the sentence in the box.**

Allow students time to find and mark their answer.

SAY: **Now look at Think It Through.**

Read Think It Through to students. Check to see that all students have filled in the correct answer space. Ask students if they have any questions.

SAY: **Now you will practice matching more words that have more than one meaning. Do numbers 1 through 4 just as we did Sample A. When you come to the stop sign at the bottom of page 49, put your pencils down. You may now begin.**

Allow students time to find and mark their answers.

Review the questions and answer choices with students. Discuss with the class why one answer is correct and the others are not correct. Also check to see that students have carefully filled in the answer spaces and have completely erased any stray marks.

## Using Context Clues

Directions: Darken the circle for the word or words that give the meaning of the underlined word, or write in the answer.

**TRY THIS** Read the first sentence carefully. Look for clue words in the sentence to help you figure out the meaning of the underlined word.

Sample A

A family finally moved into the house that has been vacant for six months. Vacant means—

- Ⓐ white
- ● empty
- Ⓒ burned
- Ⓓ built

**THINK IT THROUGH** The correct answer is B, empty. The clue words are finally moved into. All four choices have to do wih a house, but only empty has the same meaning as vacant.

STOP

1 You should not play with matches because you might harm yourself. Harm means—

- ● hurt
- Ⓑ help
- Ⓒ calm
- Ⓓ see

2 Instead of eating french fries, I ate something beneficial to my health. Beneficial means—

- Ⓕ damaging
- ● helpful
- Ⓗ equal
- Ⓙ thankful

3 The wagon train couldn't go around the river, so they had to ford it. Ford means—

- Ⓐ drain
- Ⓑ paddle
- Ⓒ fish
- ● cross

4 To observe hamsters at play, you must see them at night. Observe means—

- ● watch
- Ⓖ hear
- Ⓗ control
- Ⓙ do

5 We need a new song for our play, so our teacher will compose one. Compose means—

- Ⓐ sell
- Ⓑ hum
- ● write
- Ⓓ use

6 The instructions on the label say that you should wash that shirt in cold water. What are instructions?

*directions*



STOP

50

## Using Context Clues

Reading Skill: Using sentence context to determine word meaning

SAY: **Turn to Using Context Clues on page 50.**

Check to see that all students find page 50.

SAY: **On page 50 you will practice using clue words to help you figure out the meaning of a word.**

Read the Directions to students.

SAY: **Now look at Try This.**

Read Try This to students.

SAY: **Now look at Sample A. Read the sentence and the answer choices carefully. A family finally moved into the house that has been vacant for six months. *Vacant* means—*white ... empty ... burned ... built.* Darken the circle for the word that has the same or almost the same meaning as the underlined word, *vacant.***

Allow students time to find and mark their answer.

SAY: **Now look at Think It Through.**

Read Think It Through to students. Check to see that all students have filled in the correct answer space. Ask students if they have any questions.

SAY: **Now you will practice using clue words to figure out the meaning of more words. Do numbers 1 through 5 just as we did Sample A. For number 6, write your answer in the space provided. When you come to the stop sign at the bottom of page 50, put your pencils down. You may now begin.**

Allow students time to find and mark their answers.

Review the questions and answer choices with students. Discuss with the class why one answer is correct and the others are not correct. Also check to see that students have carefully filled in the answer spaces and have completely erased any stray marks.

## Test

Sample A

A nursery is a place for—

Ⓐ machines

Ⓑ sleds

Ⓒ nests

● babies

For questions 1–9, darken the circle for the word or words that have the same or almost the same meaning as the underlined word, or write in the answer.

1 Simple means—

Ⓐ smart

Ⓑ cheap

Ⓒ late

● easy

2 To trade something is to—

● exchange it

Ⓖ collect it

Ⓗ leave it

Ⓙ keep it

3 A kettle is a kind of—

Ⓐ food

● pot

Ⓒ chair

Ⓓ basket

4 A policy is a kind of—

● plan

Ⓖ sea bird

Ⓗ hood

Ⓙ envelope

5 Something that is accepted is—

● received

Ⓑ stolen

Ⓒ pretty

Ⓓ wrapped

6 A meadow is most like a—

Ⓕ vase

Ⓖ garden

Ⓗ store

● field

7 A yacht is a kind of—

Ⓐ deer

● boat

Ⓒ hat

Ⓓ pickle

8 To tremble means to—

Ⓕ wave

Ⓖ laugh

Ⓗ cough

● shake

9 What does it mean to slice something?

*cut*

STOP

51



# Test

SAY: **Turn to the Test on page 51.**

Check to see that all students find the Test.

SAY: **In this test you will use the reading skills that we have practiced in this unit. This test is divided into three parts. For each part there is a sample exercise. We will work each sample together. In the first part of the test, you will find words that mean the same or almost the same as the underlined word. Now look at Sample A. Read the sentence and the answer choices. A *nursery* is a place for—*machines ... sleds ... nests ... babies.* Darken the circle for the word that has the same or almost the same meaning as the underlined word, *nursery.***

Allow students time to find and mark their answer.

SAY: **You should have darkened the circle for *D, babies.***

Check to see that all students have filled in the correct answer space. Ask students if they have any questions.

SAY: **Now you will finish this part of the test on your own. Read the directions carefully. Do numbers 1 through 9 just as we did Sample A. Darken the circle for each correct answer, or write your answer in the space provided. When you come to the stop sign at the bottom of page 51, put your pencils down. You may now begin.**

Allow students time to find and mark their answers.

Sample B

| My picture hangs above the fireplace. |
|---|

**In which sentence does above have the same meaning as it does in the sentence in the box?**

- Ⓐ I had to shout above the noise.
- Ⓑ The huge flock of birds filled the skies above.
- ● Your book is on the shelf above the desk.
- Ⓓ His scores are above average.

STOP

**For questions 10–14, darken the circle for the sentence in which the underlined word means the same as it does in the sentence in the box.**

10

| The rule was fair to both teams. |
|---|

**In which sentence does fair have the same meaning as it does in the sentence above?**

- Ⓐ Let's go to the state fair.
- ● Our teacher told us to play fair.
- Ⓒ The weather today was fair.
- Ⓓ She has very fair hair.

11

| We found Grandfather's old sailor's chest in the attic. |
|---|

**In which sentence does chest have the same meaning as it does in the sentence above?**

- Ⓕ My brother caught a chest cold.
- ● My shirts are in the third drawer of my chest.
- Ⓗ The pirates put their treasure in a chest.
- Ⓙ The football hit him in the chest.

12

| Al will act the hero's part. |
|---|

**In which sentence does act have the same meaning as it does in the sentence above?**

- ● I would love to act in a movie.
- Ⓑ We liked the third act of the play.
- Ⓒ She told us to act like gentlemen.
- Ⓓ The soldier performed a brave act.

13

| Draw a picture in this space. |
|---|

**In which sentence does space have the same meaning as it does in the sentence above?**

- Ⓕ It came from outer space.
- Ⓖ Space the letters evenly on the line.
- Ⓗ A space of two weeks followed.
- ● Leave a space for your name.

14

| What time does the show start? |
|---|

**In which sentence does time have the same meaning as it does in the sentence above?**

- Ⓐ The coach will time my race.
- Ⓑ I had a good time at the party.
- Ⓒ Try to keep time with the music.
- ● It is now time to return to class.



STOP

52

SAY: **Now turn to page 52. Find Sample B.**

Check to see that all students find Sample B on page 52.

SAY: **In this part of the test, you will match words that have more than one meaning. Look at Sample B. Read the sentence in the box and the question below it. My picture hangs *above* the fireplace. In which sentence does *above* have the same meaning as it does in the sentence in the box? *I had to shout above the noise ... The huge flock of birds filled the skies above ... Your book is on the shelf above the desk ... His scores are above average.* Darken the circle for the sentence that uses the word *above* in the same way as the sentence in the box.**

Allow students time to find and mark their answers.

SAY: **You should have darkened the circle for *C*. In that sentence, *above* means "over," just as it does in the sentence in the box.**

Check to see that all students have filled in the correct answer space. Ask students if they have any questions.

SAY: **Now you will finish this part of the test on your own. Read the directions carefully. Do numbers 10 through 14 just as we did Sample B. Darken the circle for each correct answer. When you come to the stop sign at the bottom of page 52, put your pencils down. You may now begin.**

Allow students time to find and mark their answers.

**Sample C**

The unsafe trail was marked with a warning sign. Unsafe means—

Ⓐ scenic
Ⓑ hilly
● dangerous
Ⓓ winding

**For questions 15–21, darken the circle for the word or words that give the meaning of the underlined word, or write in the answer.**

15 Instead of dull gray, I wanted to paint my room vivid yellow. Vivid means—

● bright
Ⓖ dark
Ⓗ lemon
Ⓙ cool

16 If you don't want to buy a boat, you can charter one for your fishing trip. Charter means—

Ⓐ choose
Ⓑ sail
● rent
Ⓓ trade

17 We like everything in the show, but our favorite segment is the pet tricks. Segment means—

Ⓕ actor
Ⓖ song
● part
Ⓙ star

18 We tried to open the trunk, but the lid would not budge. Budge means—

Ⓐ slam
Ⓑ rest
● move
Ⓓ burn

19 Wild horses roam freely in Nevada. Roam means—

Ⓕ sleep
● wander
Ⓗ eat
Ⓙ hide

20 Because I was tired, I neglected to do my exercises. Neglected means—

Ⓐ tried
● failed
Ⓒ knew
Ⓓ meant

21 Our kite was broken, but Uncle Victor helped us repair it. Repair means—

***fix***

STOP

53



SAY: **Now turn to page 53. Find Sample C.**

Check to see that all students find Sample C on page 53.

SAY: **In this part of the test, you will use clue words to help you figure out the meaning of the underlined word. Read the sentence and the four answer choices. The *unsafe* trail was marked with a warning sign. *Unsafe* means—*scenic ... hilly ... dangerous ... winding.* Darken the circle for the word that has the same or almost the same meaning as the underlined word, *unsafe.***

Allow students time to find and mark their answers.

SAY: **You should have darkened the circle for *C*, *dangerous,* because *dangerous* means the same as *unsafe.***

Check to see that all students have filled in the correct answer space. Ask students if they have any questions.

SAY: **Now you will finish this part of the test on your own. Read the directions carefully. Do numbers 15 through 21 just as we did Sample C. Darken the circle for each correct answer, or write your answer in the space provided. When you come to the stop sign at the bottom of page 53, put your pencils down. You may now begin.**

Allow students time to find and mark their answers.

SAY: **It is now time to stop. You have completed the Test. Make sure you have carefully filled in your answer spaces and have completely erased any stray marks. Then put your pencils down.**

After the test has been scored, review the questions and answer choices with students. If students are having difficulty with any lesson, provide them with additional practice items.

UNIT FIVE

# Math Problem-Solving Strategies

## Overview

### The Problem-Solving Plan

*When solving math problems follow these steps:*

**STEP 1: WHAT IS THE QUESTION/GOAL?**
Decide what must be found. This information is usually presented in the form of a question.

**STEP 2: FIND THE FACTS**
Locate the factual information in three different ways:

A. KEY FACTS...the facts you need to solve the problem.
B. FACTS YOU DON'T NEED...those facts which are not necessary for solving the problem.
C. ARE MORE FACTS NEEDED?...decide if you have enough information to solve the problem.

**STEP 3: SELECT A STRATEGY**
Decide what you can do to solve the problem.

**STEP 4: SOLVE**
Use your plan to solve the problem.

**STEP 5: DOES YOUR RESPONSE MAKE SENSE?**
Think about your answer. Does it make sense?





# Unit 5: Math Problem-Solving Strategies

Mathematics Skills: Identifying key facts and missing information in problems; using problem-solving strategies

Distribute scratch paper to students. Tell them they may use the scratch paper to work the problems.

SAY: **Turn to Unit 5, Math Problem-Solving Strategies, on page 54.**

Check to see that all students find Unit 5.

SAY: **In Unit 5, you will practice choosing strategies, and following a five-step plan, that can be used to solve problems.**

Read the *Overview* to students.

SAY: **Now look at *Step 1*.**

Read *Step 1* to students.

SAY: **Now look at *Step 2*.**

Read *Step 2* to students.

SAY: **Now look at *Step 3*.**

Read *Step 3* to students.

SAY: **Now look at *Step 4*.**

Read *Step 4* to students.

SAY: **Now look at *Step 5*.**

Read *Step 5* to students.

SAY: **Now you will practice solving problems. Do problems 1 and 2 by following the five steps in the problem-solving plan. When you come to the bottom of page 57, put your pencils down. You may now begin.**

Allow students time to complete problems and fill-in the steps.

Review problems and steps with students. Discuss with the class how to solve problems by using logical thinking.

## Problem 1

**PROBLEM/QUESTION:**

Jackie is going shopping for presents in Green's Toy Store. Mr. Green sells toy bears for $1.98, toy dogs for $1.50, toy cats for $1.45, toy birds for $1.10 and toy snakes for $.88. She can buy only one of each toy animal. Jackie has $5.00 to spend. What is the greatest number of toys she can buy?

**STEP 1: WHAT IS THE QUESTION/GOAL?**

***What is the greatest number of toys Jackie can buy with $5.00?***

**STEP 2: FIND THE FACTS**

***Bears cost $1.98***
***Dogs cost $1.50***
***Cats cost $1.45***

***Birds cost $1.10***
***Snakes cost $.88***

***Jackie has $5.00***
***Jackie can buy no more than one of each animal.***

**STEP 3: SELECT A STRATEGY**

***Buy toys one at a time, starting with the least expensive, until there isn't enough money left to buy another toy.***

**STEP 4: SOLVE**

| *Buy the first toy* | *Buy the second toy* | *Buy the third toy* | *Buy the fourth toy* |
|---|---|---|---|
| *$5.00* | *$4.12* | *$3.02* | *$1.57* |
| *-.88* | *-1.10* | *-1.45* | *-1.50* |
| *$4.12* | *$3.02* | *$1.57* | *$.07* |

**STEP 5: DOES YOUR RESPONSE MAKE SENSE?**

***Yes, because there were on 7 cents left after the 4 least expensive toys were purchased.***

## Problem 2

**PROBLEM/QUESTION:**

Eduardo has a choice of 4 possible outfits that he can wear today. He has one striped and one solid shirt. He also has a pair of black pants and a pair of blue pants. Describe the 4 combinations of shirts and pants Eduardo can make.

**STEP 1: WHAT IS THE QUESTION/GOAL?**

***Describe the 4 outfits Eduardo can make.***

**STEP 2: FIND THE FACTS**

| ***Shirts*** | ***Pants*** |
|---|---|
| ***1 striped*** | ***1 black*** |
| ***1 solid*** | ***1 blue*** |

**STEP 3: SELECT A STRATEGY**

***Make a list of combinations of shirts and pants.***

**STEP 4: SOLVE**

| ***Outfit 1*** | ***Outfit 2*** | ***Outfit 3*** | ***Outfit 4*** |
|---|---|---|---|
| ***Striped shirt & black pants*** | ***Striped shirt & blue pants*** | ***Solid shirt & black pants*** | ***Solid shirt & blue pants*** |

**STEP 5: DOES YOUR RESPONSE MAKE SENSE?**

***Yes, because it lists 4 different outfits.***

UNIT SIX

# Math Problem Solving

## Understanding Numeration

Directions: Darken the circle for the correct answer, or write in the answer.

**TRY THIS** **Read each problem carefully. Be sure to think about which numbers stand for hundreds, tens, and ones.**

Sample A

**Which is another way to write 238?**

Ⓐ 20 + 380

● 200 + 30 + 8

Ⓒ 200 + 30 + 80

Ⓓ 2,000 + 30 + 8

**THINK IT THROUGH** **The correct answer is B. 200 + 30 + 8 = 238. Therefore, 238 = 200 + 30 + 8.**

STOP

1 **Juanita baked an odd number of muffins to take to the bake sale. How many muffins did she bake?**

● 17 muffins

Ⓑ 16 muffins

Ⓒ 12 muffins

Ⓓ 10 muffins

2

| Name | Points |
|---|---|
| Chris | 192 |
| Fatima | 150 |
| Mike | 269 |
| Gwen | 148 |

**Which child scored the most number of points in a computer game?**

*Mike*

3 **Which number belongs in the box on the number line?**

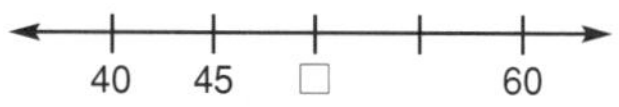


| 46 | 50 | 55 | 58 |
|---|---|---|---|
| Ⓕ | ● | Ⓗ | Ⓙ |

4 **The chart shows how long it takes to grow 4 kinds of plants.**

| Corn | Beans | Tomatoes | Peppers |
|---|---|---|---|
| 72 days | 43 days | 60 days | 54 days |

**Which group shows these plants listed in order from shortest to longest growing time?**

● beans, peppers, tomatoes, corn

Ⓑ peppers, beans, tomatoes, corn

Ⓒ corn, beans, tomatoes, peppers

Ⓓ tomatoes, peppers, beans, corn

STOP





# Unit 6: Math Problem Solving

## Understanding Numeration

Mathematics Skills: Identifying odd and even numbers; recognizing numerals; understanding place value; comparing and ordering numbers

Distribute scratch paper to students. Tell them they may use the scratch paper to work the problems.

SAY: **Turn to Understanding Numeration on page 57**

Check to see that all students find page 57.

SAY: **On page 57 you will practice solving problems with numerals, place value, and the order of numbers.**

Read the Directions to the students.

SAY: **Now look at Try This.**

Read Try This to the students.

SAY: **Now look at Sample A. Read the question carefully. You are asked to find another way to write the number 238. Look at the answer choices. Then darken the circle for the correct answer.**

Allow students time to choose and mark their answer.

SAY: **Now look at Think It Through.**

Read Think It Through to students. Check to see that all students have filled in the correct answer space. Ask students if they have any questions.

SAY: **Now you will practice solving more problems with numerals, place value, and numeral order. Do numbers 1 through 4 just as we did Sample A, or write in your answer. When you come to the stop sign at the bottom of the page, put your pencils down. You may now begin.**

Allow students time to find and mark their answers.

Review the questions and answer choices with students. Discuss with the class why one answer is correct and the others are not correct. Also check to see that students have carefully filled in their answer spaces.

## Using Whole Numbers, Fractions, and Decimals

Directions: Darken the circle for the correct answer, or write in the answer.

**TRY THIS**

**Read the question twice before choosing your answer. Try using all the answer choices back in the problem. Then choose the answer that you think best answers the question.**

Sample A

What is another way to write 4 + 4 + 4 ?

Ⓐ 3 + 4

● 3 × 4

Ⓒ 4 × 4 × 4

Ⓓ 12 + 4

**THINK IT THROUGH**

The correct answer is B, 3 × 4. 4 + 4 + 4 = 12. Choice B, 3 × 4, is the only answer which equals 12.

STOP

1 What fraction of the shape is not shaded?

$\frac{4}{5}$

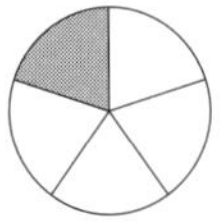

2

| Name | Number of Inches |
|---|---|
| Yoshi | 1.9 |
| Penelope | 2.1 |
| Marcus | 1.7 |
| Felicia | 2.4 |

Which child grew the most inches in a year?

Ⓐ Yoshi

Ⓑ Penelope

Ⓒ Marcus

● Felicia

3 Which number belongs in the box to make the number sentence correct?

7 × □ = 7 ?

| 7 | 6 | 1 | 0 |
|---|---|---|---|
| Ⓕ | Ⓖ | ● | Ⓙ |

4 Which number sentence is in the same fact family as

8 + 3 = 11 ?

Ⓐ 8 × 3 = 24

Ⓑ 5 + 6 = 11

● 11 − 3 = 8

Ⓓ 11 + 3 = 14

5 Which group of balloons has $\frac{1}{3}$ of the balloons shaded?

● Ⓖ Ⓗ Ⓙ

STOP





# Using Whole Numbers, Fractions, and Decimals

Mathematics Skills: Understanding families of number facts and the properties of whole numbers; understanding fundamental operations and fractional parts; comparing and ordering fractions and decimals

Distribute scratch paper to students. Tell them they may use the scratch paper to work the problems.

SAY: **Turn to Using Whole Numbers, Fractions, and Decimals, on page 58.**

Check to see that all students find page 58.

SAY: **On page 58 you will practice solving problems with whole numbers, fractions, and decimals.**

Read the Directions to the students.

SAY: **Now look at Try This.**

Read Try This to the students.

SAY: **Now look at the Sample A. You are asked to find another way to write 4 + 4 + 4. Now look at the answer choices. Darken the circle for the correct answer.**

Allow students time to choose and mark their answer. Remind students to carefully fill in the answer space and to completely erase any stray marks.

SAY: **Now look at Think It Through.**

Read Think It Through to students. Check to see that all students have filled in the correct answer space. Ask students if they have any questions.

SAY: **Now you will practice solving more problems with whole numbers, fractions, and decimals. Do numbers 1 through 5 just as we did Sample A, or write in your answer. When you come to the stop sign at the bottom of the page, put your pencils down. You may now begin.**

Allow students time to find and mark their answers.

Review the questions and answer choices with students. Discuss with the class why one answer is correct and the others are not correct. Also check to see that students have carefully filled in their answer spaces.

## Understanding Patterns and Relationships

**Directions: Darken the circle for the correct answer, or write in the answer.**

**TRY THIS** — **Read each question carefully. Look at each answer choice to see which number or figure will answer the question correctly.**

**Sample A**

**What missing number completes the pattern in the boxes?**

| 46 | 42 | 38 | 34 | |
|---|---|---|---|---|

● 30 Ⓒ 33
Ⓑ 32 Ⓓ 35

**THINK IT THROUGH** — **The correct answer is A, 30. The numbers in the pattern decrease by 4. So, the correct answer is 30, because 34 – 4 = 30.**

STOP

**1** **Which of these shows the missing piece of the figure?**

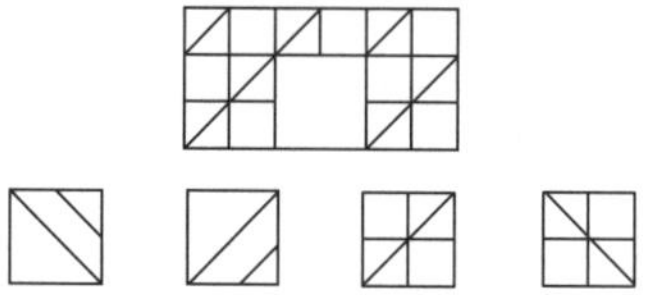

Ⓐ Ⓑ ● Ⓓ

**2** **Which of these shows the missing piece of the figure?**

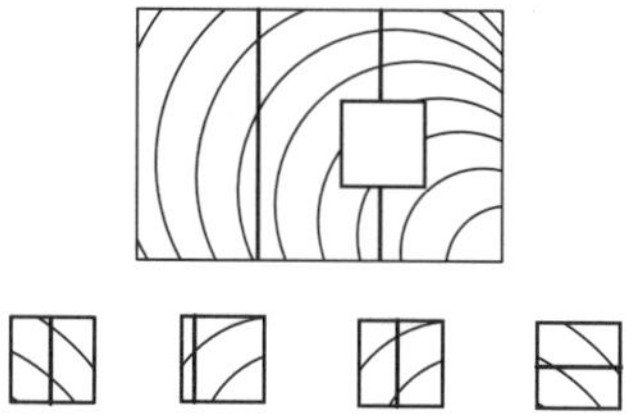

Ⓕ Ⓖ ● Ⓙ

**3** **What missing number completes the pattern in the boxes?**

| 73 | 75 | 77 | | 81 |
|---|---|---|---|---|

Ⓐ 77 ● 79
Ⓑ 78 Ⓓ 80

**4** **Each juice carton holds 6 drinks. What missing number completes the pattern in the chart?**

| Number of Drinks | |
|---|---|
| Number of Cartons of Grape Juice | Number of Drinks |
| 2 | 12 |
| 3 | 18 |
| 4 | ? |
| 5 | 30 |

*24*

STOP





# Understanding Patterns and Relationships

Mathematics Skills: Recognizing and interpreting number patterns and geometric patterns

Distribute scratch paper to students. Tell them they may use the scratch paper to work the problems.

SAY: **Turn to Understanding Patterns and Relationships on page 59.**

Check to see that all students find page 59.

SAY: **On page 59 you will practice solving problems with number patterns and relationships.**

Read the Directions to the students.

SAY: **Now look at Try This.**

Read Try This to the students.

SAY: **Now look at Sample A. You are asked to find the number that will complete the number pattern. Study the numbers in the boxes. Look at the answer choices. Which number completes the pattern? Darken the circle next to the correct answer.**

Allow students time to choose and mark their answer.

SAY: **Now look at Think It Through.**

Read Think It Through to students. Check to see that all students have filled in the correct answer space. Ask students if they have any questions.

SAY: **Now you will practice solving more problems with number patterns and relationships. Do numbers 1 through 3 just as we did Sample A. For number 4, write in your answer. When you come to the stop sign at the bottom of the page, put your pencils down. You may now begin.**

Allow students time to find and mark their answers.

Review the questions and answer choices with students. Discuss with the class why one answer is correct and the others are not correct. Also check to see that students have carefully filled in their answer spaces and have completely erased any stray marks.

## Working with Statistics and Probability

Directions: Darken the circle for the correct answer, or write in the answer.

**TRY THIS** Look at each chart, graph, or picture. Then read the question carefully. Look for words or numbers in the question that tell you what information to find.

Sample A

The tally chart shows the number of pounds of litter Kyle collected on a cleanup project.

How many pounds of paper did Kyle collect?

Ⓐ 2
Ⓑ 7
Ⓒ 8
● 10

**Litter Collected**

| | |
|---|---|
| Paper | 𝍸 𝍸 |
| Metal | 𝍸 |
| Plastic | 𝍸 𝍷𝍷 |
| Cloth | 𝍷𝍷 |
| Other | 𝍸 𝍷 |

**THINK IT THROUGH** The correct answer Is D, 10. Each tally mark stands for 1 pound of paper. Each group of 4 tally marks with a slash stands for 5 pounds of paper. Since there are 2 groups, 5 + 5 = 10 pounds of paper.

STOP

The graph below shows the pets owned by students in Mr. Ito's class. Study the graph and answer questions 1 and 2.

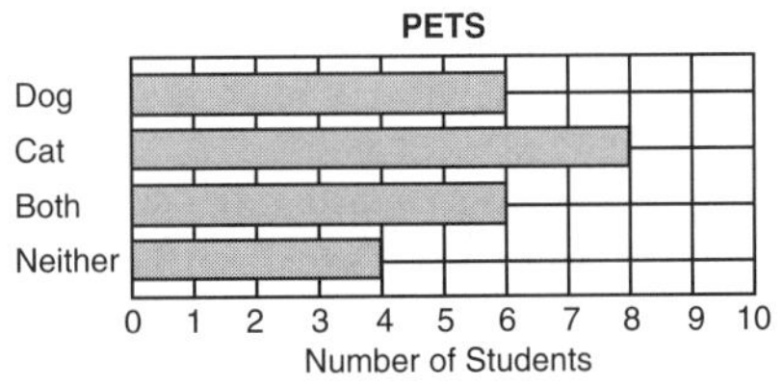


1 Which pet was the most popular?

Ⓐ Dog
● Cat
Ⓒ Both
Ⓓ Neither

2 How many more students owned cats than dogs?

● 2
Ⓖ 3
Ⓗ 5
Ⓙ 6

3 Dan is using a spinner. Which color will he be the least likely to spin?

*blue*

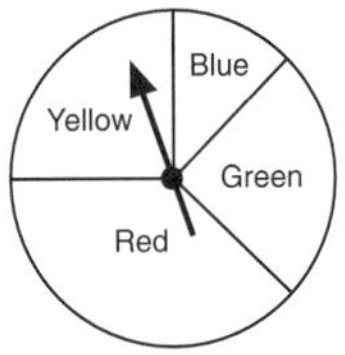


GO ON

60



# Working with Statistics and Probability

Mathematics Skills: Reading and interpreting bar graphs, tables, and tally charts; determining simple probability

SAY: **Turn to Working with Statistics and Probability on page 60.**

Check to see that all students find page 60.

SAY: **On page 60 you will practice solving statistics problems using graphs, tables, and tally charts, and working with probability problems.**

Read the Directions to the students.

SAY: **Now look at Try This.**

Read Try This to the students.

SAY: **Now look at Sample A. You are asked to find information in a tally chart. Study the tally chart carefully. How many pounds of paper did Kyle collect? Darken the circle for the correct answer.**

Allow students time to choose and mark their answer.

SAY: **Now look at Think It Through.**

Read Think It Through to students. Check to see that all students have filled in the correct answer space. Ask students if they have any questions.

SAY: **Now you will practice solving more statistics and probability problems. Do numbers 1 through 7 just as we did Sample A, or write in your answer. When you come to the arrow and the words *GO ON* at the bottom of page 60, continue working on the next page. When you come to the stop sign at the bottom of page 61, put your pencils down. You may now begin.**

Allow students time to find and mark their answers.

4 **The students in Ms. Iannatti's class made this chart to count the fruit they ate in one day.**

| Fruit | Number Eaten |
|---|---|
| Bananas | 8 |
| Plums | 2 |
| Oranges | 12 |
| Apples | 16 |
| Peaches | 4 |

**Which kind of fruit did students eat exactly 2 times as many of as bananas?**

Ⓐ Peaches

Ⓑ Bananas

Ⓒ Oranges

● Apples

5 **The tally chart shows the favorite subjects of the students in Mrs. Fine's class.**

**Favorite Subject for Third Grade Students**

| | |
|---|---|
| Science | \|\|\| |
| Social Studies | ~~\|\|\|\|~~ \| |
| Math | ~~\|\|\|\|~~ \|\|\|\| |
| Language | ~~\|\|\|\|~~ \|\|\| |

**How many students liked language?**

Ⓕ 3

Ⓖ 6

● 8

Ⓙ 9

6 **Look at the cards shown here.**

C D D B D

A D C D D

**If Kevin picks a card without looking, which will he most likely choose?**

Ⓐ A

Ⓑ B

Ⓒ C

● D

7 **Ellen collected these shells in a bucket.**

| | |
|---|---|
|  | **3** |
|  | **12** |
|  | **2** |
|  | **4** |

**If she picks 1 shell out of the bucket without looking, which kind will it most likely be?**

 Ⓕ

 ●

 Ⓗ

 Ⓙ

STOP

## Understanding Geometry

Directions: Darken the circle for the correct answer, or write in the answer.

**TRY THIS** Read each question carefully. Study the objects named or shown and use them to help you to choose the correct answer.

Sample A

Which figure will have two halves that match exactly when it is folded on the solid line?

Ⓐ Ⓑ ● Ⓓ

**THINK IT THROUGH** The correct choice is C. If the heart is folded on the solid line, each half will match exactly.

STOP

1 Everyone at Shari's birthday party wore a party hat like the one shown here. What shape does the hat have?

● cone
Ⓑ pyramid
Ⓒ cube
Ⓓ sphere

2 Look at the numbered shapes. Which two are exactly the same in size and shape?

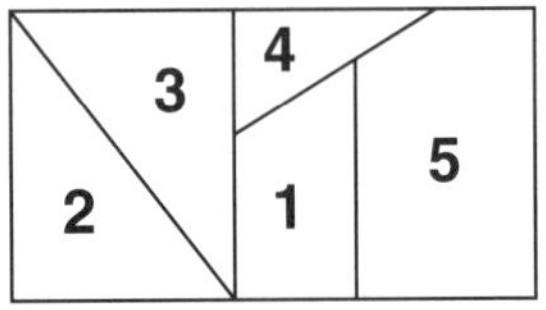


*2 and 3*

3 Which shape has four corners and four sides exactly the same size?

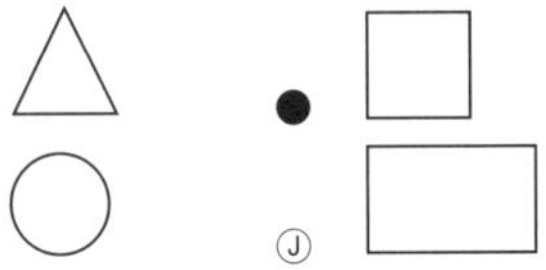

Ⓕ ● Ⓖ Ⓙ

4 Moira drew this figure on her paper.

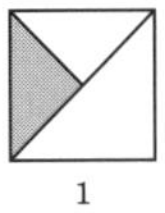

What did it look like when she turned it upside down?

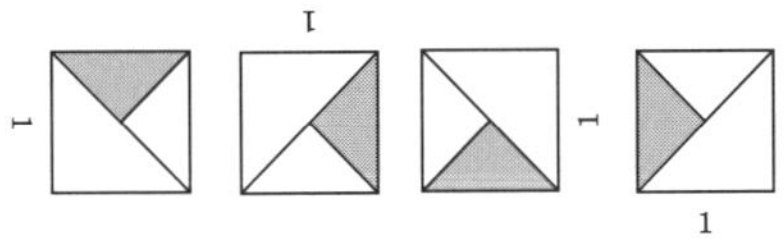

Ⓐ ● Ⓒ Ⓓ

STOP

62



# Understanding Geometry

Mathematics Skills: Recognizing geometric shapes; understanding basic properties of plane figures and rotations; identifying congruent figures and common solid figures

Distribute scratch paper to students. Tell them they may use the scratch paper to work the problems.

SAY: **Turn to Understanding Geometry on page 62.**

Check to see that all students find page 62.

SAY: **On page 62 you will practice solving problems with shapes and figures.**

Read the Directions to the students.

SAY: **Now look at Try This.**

Read Try This to the students.

SAY: **Now look at Sample A. You are asked which figure will have two halves that match exactly when folded on the solid line. Darken the circle for the correct answer.**

Allow students time to choose and mark their answer.

SAY: **Now look at Think It Through.**

Read Think It Through to students. Check to see that all students have filled in the correct answer space. Ask students if they have any questions.

SAY: **Now you will practice solving more problems using shapes and figures. Do numbers 1 through 4 just as we did Sample A, or write in your answer. When you come to the stop sign at the bottom of the page, put your pencils down. You may now begin.**

Allow students time to find and mark their answers.

Review the questions and answer choices with students. Discuss with the class why one answer is correct and the others are not correct. Also check to see that students have carefully filled in their answer spaces and have completely erased any stray marks.

## Working with Measurement

Directions: Darken the circle for the correct answer, or write in the answer.

**TRY THIS** Look at each picture or object shown. Then read the question carefully. Look for words or numbers in the question that tell you what information to find.

Sample A

Cliff ate lunch at 12:00 noon. He went to the park one and one-half hours later. Which clock shows the time Cliff went to the park?

Ⓐ 

Ⓒ 

Ⓑ 

● 

**THINK IT THROUGH** The correct answer is D, 1:30 P.M. If Cliff ate lunch at 12:00 noon, an hour and one-half hour later is 1:30 P.M.

STOP

1 Use your centimeter ruler to help answer this question.

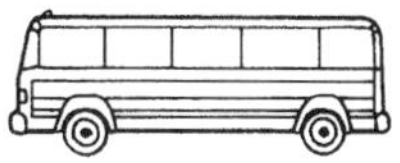

How many centimeters long is the toy bus?

*4 centimeters*

2 Which unit of measurement is best to use to describe the amount of juice in a jar?

● cups　Ⓒ pounds
Ⓑ inches　Ⓓ teaspoons

3 Monica found a dime, a nickel, and a quarter in her coat pocket.

What is the value of the money shown?

Ⓕ 45¢　Ⓗ 36¢
● 40¢　Ⓙ 31¢

GO ON





# Working with Measurement

Mathematics Skills: Identifying units of measurement; measuring and comparing units of time, length, and area using standard and nonstandard measurement units; determining the value of currency; understanding currency exchange

Distribute scratch paper to students. Tell them they may use the scratch paper to work the problems. Distribute inch and centimeter rulers to students or make sure students have these rulers. Tell them they may use the rulers to solve some problems.

SAY: **Turn to Working with Measurement on page 63.**

Check to see that all students find page 63.

SAY: **On page 63 you will practice solving problems about measurement.**

Read the Directions to the students.

SAY: **Now look at Try This.**

Read Try This to the students.

SAY: **Now look at Sample A. You are asked which clock shows the time Cliff went to the park? Darken the circle for the correct answer.**

Allow students time to choose and mark their answer.

SAY: **Now look at Think It Through.**

Read Think It Through to students. Check to see that all students have filled in the correct answer space. Ask students if they have any questions.

SAY: **Now you will practice solving more problems about measurement. Do numbers 1 through 7 just as we did Sample A, or write in your answer. When you come to the arrow and the words *GO ON* at the bottom of page 63, continue working on the next page. When you come to the stop sign at the bottom of page 64, put your pencils down. You may now begin.**

Allow students time to find and mark their answers.

4 **Marc bought a package of drawing paper that cost 59¢. He gave the clerk 75¢. How much change should Marc get back?**

Ⓐ 

● 

Ⓒ 

Ⓓ 

5 **Jennifer is going to shovel snow off the sidewalk. What is the temperature like outside?**

Ⓕ 92°

Ⓖ 75°

Ⓗ 51°

● 30°

6 **Mrs. Traub feeds the animals who live behind her house. Which animal lives the shortest distance from Mrs. Traub's house?**

Ⓐ Ⓑ ● Ⓓ

7 **Terrell drew 2 lines. Use your inch ruler to measure the total length of the lines.**

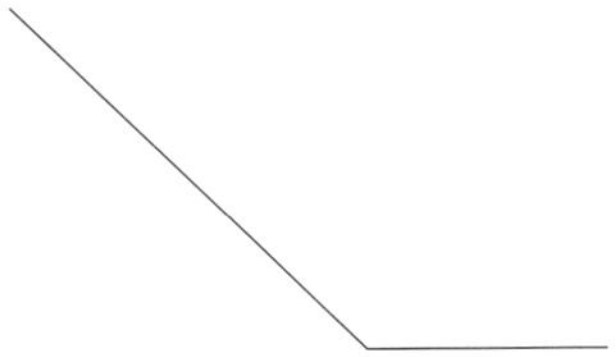

Ⓕ 1 inch

Ⓖ 2 inches

● 3 inches

Ⓙ 4 inches



STOP



Review the questions and answer choices with students. Discuss with the class why one answer is correct and the others are not correct. Also check to see that students have carefully filled in their answer spaces and have completely erased any stray marks.

## Solving Problems

Directions: Darken the circle for the correct answer, or write in the answer.

**TRY THIS** Study the words in each problem carefully. Then decide what you have to do to find the answer.

Sample A

Igor blew up 4 fewer balloons than Andy. Andy blew up 6 balloons more than Betsy. Betsy blew up 10 balloons. How many balloons did Igor blow up?

Ⓐ 20

Ⓑ 16

● 12

Ⓓ 8

**THINK IT THROUGH** The correct answer Is C, 12. Betsy blew up 10 balloons. If Andy blew up 6 more than Betsy, he blew up 16 (10 + 6). If Igor blew up 4 fewer than Andy, he blew up 12, since 16 – 4 = 12.

STOP

1 Michelle caught 9 fish. She put all of the small fish back into the water. What do you need to know to find out how many fish Michelle took home?

*how many fish Michelle put into the water*

2 There are 4 tour vans at the restaurant. The 32 people on the tour stopped to eat dinner. Which is the most reasonable answer for how many people rode in each van?

Ⓐ 128

Ⓑ 36

Ⓒ 28

● 8

3 Marvin collected 45 cans for recycling. Ira collected 39 cans. Which number sentence shows how to find the number of cans they collected altogether?

Ⓕ 39 + n = 45

Ⓖ 45 – 39 = n

Ⓗ 45 – n = 39

● 45 + 39 = n

4 What number is inside the triangle, inside the square, and is an odd number?

Ⓐ 2

Ⓑ 5

Ⓒ 7

● 9

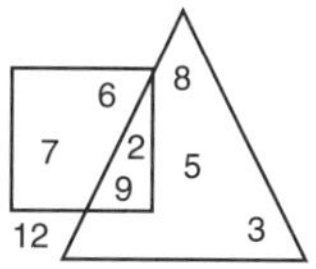


STOP

65



# Solving Problems

Mathematics Skills: Determining solution sentences for fundamental operations; identifying missing information; using estimation in problem solving; identifying reasonableness; solving problems using logic

Distribute scratch paper to students. Tell them they may use the scratch paper to work the problems.

SAY: **Turn to Solving Problems on page 65.**

Check to see that all students find page 65.

SAY: **On page 65 you will practice solving word problems and estimation problems.**

Read the Directions to the students.

SAY: **Now look at Try This.**

Read Try This to the students.

SAY: **Now look at Sample A. You are asked to find how many balloons Igor blew up. Darken the circle for the correct answer.**

Allow students time to choose and mark their answer.

SAY: **Now look at Think It Through.**

Read Think It Through to students. Check to see that all students have filled in the correct answer space. Ask students if they have any questions.

SAY: **Now you will practice solving more word problems and estimation problems. Do numbers 1 through 4 just as we did Sample A, or write in your answer. When you come to the stop sign at the bottom of the page, put your pencils down. You may now begin.**

Allow students time to find and mark their answers.

Review the questions and answer choices with students. Discuss with the class why one answer is correct and the others are not correct. Also check to see that students have carefully filled in their answer spaces and have completely erased any stray marks.

## Math Procedures
## Understanding Computation

Directions: Darken the circle for the correct answer. If the correct answer is not given, darken the circle for NH for not here.

**TRY THIS** Study each problem carefully. Look at the sign to know if you should add, subtract, multiply, or divide. Then work the problem on scratch paper. Be sure to line up the digits. Remember to regroup where necessary.

Sample A

15 − □ = 8

| A | B | C | D | E |
|---|---|---|---|---|
| 23 | 10 | 8 | 7 ● | NH |

**THINK IT THROUGH** The correct answer is D, 7. To find the missing number, subtract 8 from 15 to get the answer, 7.

STOP

1. 6)48

| A | B | C | D | E |
|---|---|---|---|---|
| 8 ● | 7 | 6 | 5 | NH |

2. 9 ÷ 3 = □

| F | G | H | J | K |
|---|---|---|---|---|
| 6 | 5 | 4 | 3 ● | NH |

3. 22 + 21

| A | B | C | D | E |
|---|---|---|---|---|
| 42 | 41 | 39 | 24 | NH ● |

4. 30 + 184 + 76

| F | G | H | J | K |
|---|---|---|---|---|
| 115 | 124 | 290 ● | 560 | NH |

5. 6 × 3

| A | B | C | D | E |
|---|---|---|---|---|
| 24 | 18 ● | 12 | 9 | NH |

6. 92 − 57

| F | G | H | J | K |
|---|---|---|---|---|
| 35 ● | 39 | 45 | 149 | NH |

7. 549 + 81

| A | B | C | D | E |
|---|---|---|---|---|
| 620 | 630 ● | 720 | 730 | NH |

8. 403 × 3

| F | G | H | J | K |
|---|---|---|---|---|
| 1,206 | 1,248 | 3,208 | 3,248 | NH ● |



STOP

66

# Math Procedures

## Understanding Computation

Mathematics Skills: Adding, subtracting, multiplying, and dividing whole numbers

Distribute scratch paper to students. Tell them they may use the scratch paper to work the problems.

SAY: **Turn to Understanding Computation on page 66.**

Check to see that all students find page 66.

SAY: **On page 66 you will practice adding, subtracting, multiplying, and dividing.**

Read the Directions to the students.

SAY: **Now look at Try This.**

Read Try This to the students.

SAY: **Look at Sample A. You are asked to find the number that makes the number sentence 15 - □ = 8, correct. Work the problem, then darken the circle for the correct answer. If the correct answer is not given, darken the circle for *NH, not here.***

Allow students time to find and mark their answer.

SAY: **Now look at Think It Through.**

Read Think It Through to students. Check to see that all students have filled in the correct answer space. Ask students if they have any questions.

SAY: **Now you will practice solving more computation problems. Do numbers 1 through 8 just as we did the Sample A. When you come to the stop sign at the bottom of the page, put your pencils down. You may now begin.**

Allow students time to find and mark their answers.

Review the questions and answer choices with students. Discuss with the class why one answer is correct and the others are not correct. Also check to see that students have carefully filled in their answer spaces and have completely erased any stray marks.

## Using Computation

Directions: Darken the circle for the correct answer. If the correct answer is not given, darken the circle for NH for not here. If no choices are given, write in the answer.

**TRY THIS** Read each problem carefully. Think about what the question is asking. Think about which numbers stand for ones, tens, and hundreds. Work the problem on scratch paper. Regroup where necessary.

Sample A

Tracey is reading a book that has 464 pages. She has read 379 pages. How many pages does she have left to read?

Ⓐ 80
● 85
Ⓒ 90
Ⓓ 95
Ⓔ NH

**THINK IT THROUGH** The correct answer is B, 85. The words "pages left to read" means to subtract 379 from 464 to get 85.

1 Eric played a computer game for 17 minutes. He played another game for 14 minutes. How many minutes did Eric play the games altogether?

| 3 | 21 | 31 | 41 | NH |
|---|---|---|---|---|
| Ⓐ | Ⓑ | ● | Ⓓ | Ⓔ |

2 Perry bought 3 boxes of crayons. There were 6 crayons in each box.

How many crayons did Perry buy altogether?

*18*

3 On Saturday, 364 children went to the park to celebrate Earth Day.

What is 364 rounded to the nearest hundred?

Ⓕ 300
Ⓖ 350
Ⓗ 360
● 400
Ⓚ NH

4 Mrs. Martin had a pizza party for her class. She wrote down the order for the pizzas.

| Cheese | Pepperoni | Vegetable |
|---|---|---|
| 8 | 5 | 2 |

How many pizzas did she buy altogether?

| 16 | 15 | 14 | 13 | NH |
|---|---|---|---|---|
| Ⓐ | ● | Ⓒ | Ⓓ | Ⓔ |





# Using Computation

Mathematics Skills: Rounding; adding and subtracting whole numbers, decimals, and money in context; multiplying whole numbers in context

Distribute scratch paper to students. Tell them they may use the scratch paper to work the problems.

SAY: **Turn to Using Computation on page 67.**

Check to see that all students find page 67.

SAY: **On page 67 you will practice solving word problems using rounding, addition, subtraction, multiplication, and division.**

Read the Directions to the students.

SAY: **Now look at Try This.**

Read Try This to the students.

SAY: **Look at Sample A. Tracy is reading a book that has 464 pages. She has read 379 pages. How many pages does she have left to read? Darken the circle for the correct answer. If the correct answer is not given, darken the circle for *NH, not here.***

Allow students time to find and mark their answer.

SAY: **Now look at Think It Through.**

Read Think It Through to students. Check to see that all students have filled in the correct answer space. Ask students if they have any questions.

SAY: **Now you will practice solving more word problems. Do numbers 1 through 4 just as we did Sample A, or write in the correct answer. When you come to the stop sign at the bottom of the page, put your pencils down. You may now begin.**

Allow students time to find and mark their answers.

Review the questions and answer choices with students. Discuss with the class why one answer is correct and the others are not correct. Also check to see that students have carefully filled in their answer spaces and have completely erased any stray marks.

## Test

**Sample A**

$$51 \times 2$$

| 52 | 53 | 72 | 102 | NH |
|---|---|---|---|---|
| Ⓐ | Ⓑ | Ⓒ | ● | Ⓔ |

STOP

**Sample B**

Jagdesh bought 12 blue balloons and 14 red balloons. How many balloons did she pick in all?

| 28 | 26 | 22 | 2 | NH |
|---|---|---|---|---|
| Ⓕ | ● | Ⓗ | Ⓙ | Ⓚ |

STOP

**For questions 1–14, darken the circle for the correct answer. If the correct answer is not here, darken the circle for NH. If no choices are given, write in the answer.**

1 $32 \div 8 = \square$

| 5 | 4 | 3 | 2 | NH |
|---|---|---|---|---|
| Ⓐ | ● | Ⓒ | Ⓓ | Ⓔ |

2 $4 \times 21 = \square$

| 25 | 62 | 80 | 84 | NH |
|---|---|---|---|---|
| Ⓕ | Ⓖ | Ⓗ | ● | Ⓚ |

3 $6 \times 5 = \square$

| 11 | 24 | 30 | 36 | NH |
|---|---|---|---|---|
| Ⓐ | Ⓑ | ● | Ⓓ | Ⓔ |

4 $315 + 23$

| 328 | 338 | 518 | 545 | NH |
|---|---|---|---|---|
| Ⓕ | ● | Ⓗ | Ⓙ | Ⓚ |

5 $200 - 164$

| 36 | 46 | 136 | 146 | NH |
|---|---|---|---|---|
| ● | Ⓑ | Ⓒ | Ⓓ | Ⓔ |

6 $460 \times 3$

| 790 | 1,180 | 1,380 | 1,383 | NH |
|---|---|---|---|---|
| Ⓕ | Ⓖ | ● | Ⓙ | Ⓚ |

7 $9\overline{)72}$

*8*

8 There were 43 pictures sent to an art contest.

What is this number rounded to the nearest ten?

| 40 | 45 | 50 | 55 | NH |
|---|---|---|---|---|
| ● | Ⓑ | Ⓒ | Ⓓ | Ⓔ |

GO ON





# Test

Distribute scratch paper to students. Tell them they may use the scratch paper to work the problems.

SAY: **Turn to the Test on page 68.**

Check to see that all students find the Test.

SAY: **In this test you will use the mathematics skills that we have practiced in this unit. Look at Sample A. You are asked to multiply 51 by 2. Work the problem, then darken the circle for the correct answer. If the correct answer is not given, darken the circle for *NH, not here.***

Allow students time to find and mark their answer.

SAY: **You should have darkened the circle for *D, 102,* because 51 x 2 = *102.***

SAY: **Now look at Sample B. Jagdesh bought 12 blue balloons and 14 red balloons. How many balloons did she pick in all? Darken the circle for the correct answer. If the correct answer is not given, darken the circle for *NH, not here.***

Allow students time to find and mark their answer.

SAY: **You should have darkened the circle for *G, 26.* You need to add 12 and 14 to find that Jagdesh picked *26* balloons in all.**

Check to see that all students have filled in the correct answer spaces. Ask students if they have any questions.

SAY: **Now you will finish the test on your own. Do numbers 1 through 14 just as we did the samples. Read the problems and the answer choices carefully. Then darken the circle for each correct answer, or write in the answer. If the correct answer is not given, darken the circle for *NH, not here.* When you come to the arrow and the words *GO ON* at the bottom of page 68, continue working on the next page. When you come to the stop sign at the bottom of page 69, put your pencils down. You may now begin.**

Allow students time to find and mark their answers.

9 At Talfourd Elementary, 687 children ride buses to school. About how many children ride buses if the number is rounded to the nearest hundred?

| 600 | 680 | 690 | 700 | NH |
|---|---|---|---|---|
| Ⓕ | Ⓖ | Ⓗ | ● | Ⓚ |

10 Dottie sewed buttons on a shirt. There were 5 buttons on each card. She had 3 cards. How many buttons did Dottie sew on the shirt?

| 18 | 15 | 8 | 2 | NH |
|---|---|---|---|---|
| Ⓐ | ● | Ⓒ | Ⓓ | Ⓔ |

11 Suki bought a ball for $3.55. She paid $0.20 tax.

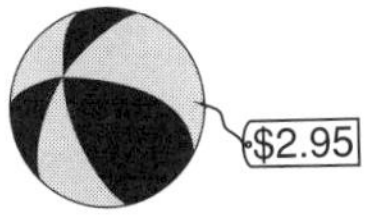


How much did Suki spend altogether?

***$3.75***

12 Hsu paid $3.29 for a box of paints.

She gave the clerk 5 $1.00 bills.

If there was no tax, how much change should Hsu receive?

| $2.81 | $2.71 | $1.81 | $1.71 | NH |
|---|---|---|---|---|
| Ⓕ | Ⓖ | Ⓗ | ● | Ⓚ |

13 Mr. Jones had to drive 380 miles to visit his brother. He had driven 189 miles by lunch. How many more miles does Mr. Jones have to drive?

Ⓐ 211
Ⓑ 201
● 191
Ⓓ 91
Ⓔ NH

14 Phoebe had saved $8.50. She earned $3.50 feeding a neighbor's cat. How much money does Phoebe have in all?

| $12.50 | $12.00 | $11.50 | $11.00 | NH |
|---|---|---|---|---|
| Ⓕ | ● | Ⓗ | Ⓙ | Ⓚ |

STOP

69



SAY: **It is now time to stop. You have completed the Test. Make sure you have carefully filled in your answer spaces and have completely erased any stray marks. Then put your pencils down.**

After the test has been scored, review the questions and answer choices with students. If students are having difficulty with any lesson, provide them with additional practice.

## Test

Sample A

Which number belongs in the box to make the number sentence correct?

□ × 1 = 24

Ⓐ 2

Ⓑ 4

Ⓒ 23

● 24

For questions 1-44, darken the circle for the correct answer, or write in the answer.

1 Harvey has 1,354 baseball cards in his collection. What is the value of the 3 in 1,354?

Ⓐ three thousand

● three hundred

Ⓒ thirty

Ⓓ three

2 The students in Mr. Lee's class are reading books. The table shows the fraction of the book each student has read.

| Name | Amount Read |
|---|---|
| Amy | $\frac{1}{5}$ |
| Jay | $\frac{1}{4}$ |
| Meiko | $\frac{1}{8}$ |
| Ross | $\frac{1}{3}$ |

Which student read the most?

Ⓕ Amy

Ⓖ Jay

Ⓗ Meiko

● Ross

3 Which is another way to write 300 + 50 + 2?

● 352

Ⓑ 3,052

Ⓒ 30,502

Ⓓ 300,502

4 Which number sentence is in the same fact family as

11 – 4 = 7

Ⓕ 11 + 4 = 15

● 7 + 4 = 11

Ⓗ 7 – 4 = 3

Ⓙ 7 × 4 = 28

5 Which is another name for eight thousand four hundred ninety-two?

● 8,492

Ⓑ 80,492

Ⓒ 84,920

Ⓓ 840,092

6 Andy has an odd number of coins in his coin collection. Which is Andy's coin collection?

Ⓕ Ⓖ ● Ⓙ

7 Which number belongs in the box on the number line?

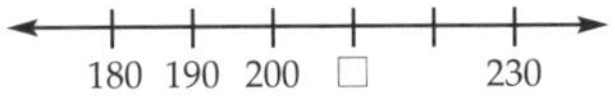


*210*

8 Which muffin pan is $\frac{1}{2}$ empty?

Ⓐ 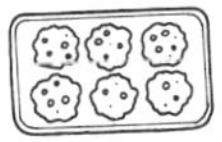

Ⓑ 

Ⓒ 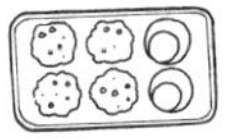

● 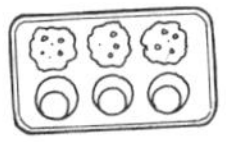



GO ON

70

# Test

Distribute scratch paper to students. Tell them they may use the scratch paper to work the problems.

Distribute inch and centimeter rulers to students or make sure they have these rulers. Tell them they may use the rulers to solve some problems.

SAY: **Turn to the Test on page 70.**

Check to see that all students find the Test.

SAY: **In this test you will use the mathematics skills that we have practiced in this unit. Look at Sample A. You are asked to tell which number will make the number sentence correct. Read the four answer choices. Darken the circle for the correct answer.**

Allow students time to find and mark their answer.

SAY: **You should have darkened the circle for *D*, the number *24*, because 24 x 1 = 24.**

Check to see that all students have filled in the correct answer spaces. Ask students if they have any questions.

SAY: **Now you will solve more math problems. Read each question carefully. Then choose your answer from the choices given for each problem. Do numbers 1 through 44 just as we did Sample A. If no choices are given, then write in your answer. When you come to the arrow and the words *GO ON* at the bottom of a page, continue working on the next page. When you come to the stop sign at the bottom of page 77, put your pencils down. You may now begin.**

Allow students time to find and mark their answers.

9 **Which number belongs in the box to make the number sentence correct?**

6 × □ = 7 × 6

Ⓕ 42
● 7
Ⓖ 13
Ⓙ 4

10 **What fraction of the shape is shaded?**

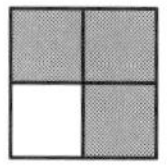

Ⓐ $\frac{1}{4}$
Ⓒ $\frac{3}{3}$
● $\frac{3}{4}$
Ⓓ $\frac{1}{3}$

11 **The table shows the number of lunches sold in the cafeteria in one week.**

| Day | Lunches |
|---|---|
| Monday | 298 |
| Tuesday | 329 |
| Wednesday | 285 |
| Thursday | 351 |
| Friday | 246 |

**On which day were the most lunches sold?**

Ⓕ Monday
Ⓗ Wednesday
Ⓖ Tuesday
● Thursday

12 **The pet store sells 4 fish for $1. What is the missing number that completes the pattern in the chart?**

| Fish to Buy | |
|---|---|
| Number of Dollars | Number of Fish |
| $ 2 | 8 |
| $ 3 | 12 |
| $ 4 | ? |
| $ 5 | 20 |

● 16
Ⓒ 13
Ⓑ 14
Ⓓ 4

13 **The chart below shows how much 4 bags of cookies weigh.**

| Cookie | Weight |
|---|---|
| Chocolate chip | 2.2 lbs. |
| Fruit bars | 1.7 lbs. |
| Ginger snaps | 2.5 lbs. |
| Oatmeal | 1.9 lbs. |

**Which cookie bag weighs the least?**

Ⓕ Chocolate chip
Ⓗ Ginger snaps
● Fruit bars
Ⓙ Oatmeal

14 **Which of these shows the missing piece in the figure?**

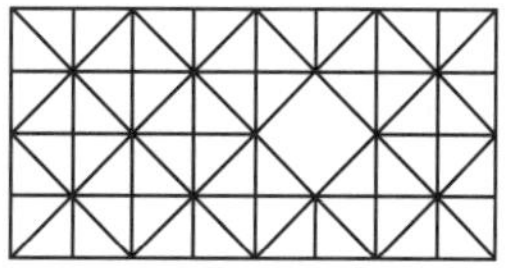

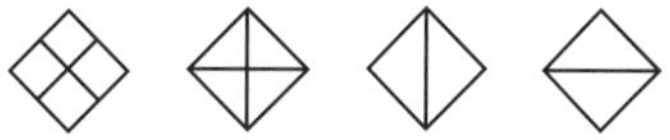

Ⓐ ● Ⓒ Ⓓ



GO ON

15 **The table shows rainfall amounts in 4 cities in Texas.**

| City | Rain Per Year |
|---|---|
| Austin | 30 inches |
| Dallas | 35 inches |
| Fort Worth | 35 inches |
| Houston | 42 inches |

**Which two cities together receive a total of 72 inches of rain a year?**

- Ⓕ Austin and Dallas
- Ⓖ Dallas and Houston
- Ⓗ Fort Worth and Dallas
- ● Austin and Houston

16 **What is the missing number that completes the pattern in the boxes?**

| | | | | |
|---|---|---|---|---|
| 19 | 15 | 11 | 7 | |

- Ⓐ 8
- Ⓑ 6
- Ⓒ 4
- ● 3

17 **The tally chart keeps track of the boxes of seeds Rebecca sells.**

| Kinds of Seeds | Boxes Sold |
|---|---|
| Flower Seeds | 卌 卌 |
| Vegetable Seeds | 卌 \|\|\| |
| Herb Seeds | 卌 \| |
| Birdseed | \|\|\|\| |

**How many boxes of vegetable seeds did Rebecca sell?**

- Ⓕ 2
- Ⓖ 4
- Ⓗ 6
- ● 8

**The graph below shows the shoes students are wearing in Mrs. Fryman's class. Study the graph and answer questions 18 through 20.**

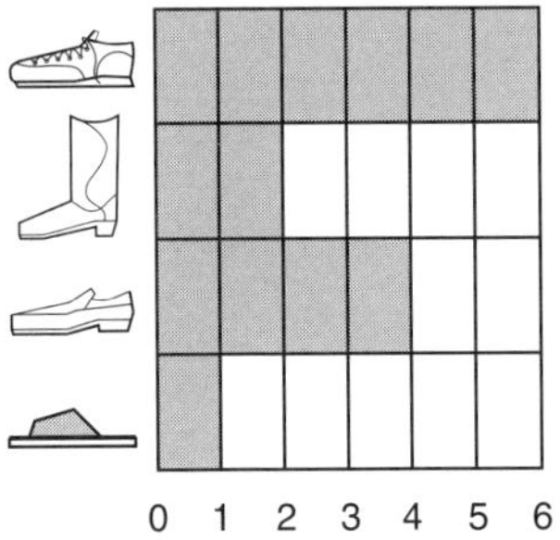


18 **How many students are wearing sandals and boots?**

- Ⓐ 1
- Ⓑ 2
- ● 3
- Ⓓ 6

19 **Which category shows the shoes that 4 students are wearing?**

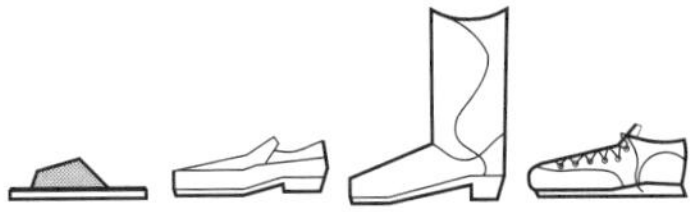

Ⓕ ● Ⓗ Ⓙ

20 **How many more students are wearing shoes than boots?**

*2*



GO ON

21 **What shape does the ball have?**

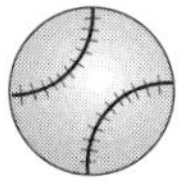

Ⓐ pyramid

Ⓑ cone

● sphere

Ⓓ cube

22 **What is the location of the**  **?**

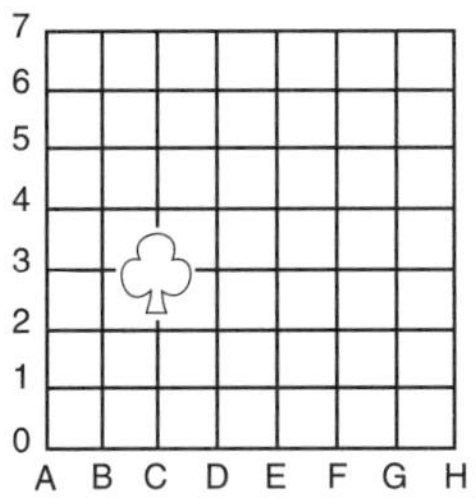


| B4 | C3 | F5 | D1 |
|---|---|---|---|
| Ⓕ | ● | Ⓗ | Ⓙ |

23 **Look at the numbered shapes. Which two figures are exactly the same in size and shape?**

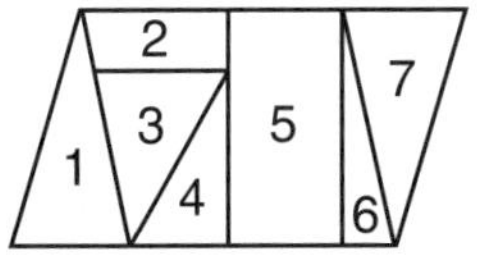


Ⓐ 1 and 4

Ⓑ 2 and 5

● 1 and 7

Ⓓ 4 and 6

24 **These shapes were picked out of a box.**

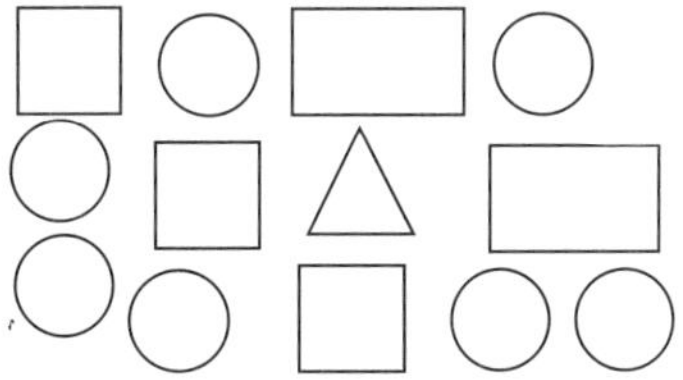

**If one more shape is picked from the box, which shape will it most likely be?**

● 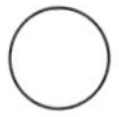 Ⓗ 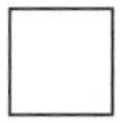

Ⓖ 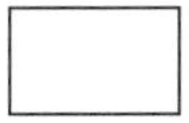 Ⓙ 

25 **Terry is playing a game with the spinner. Which number will the next spin most likely show?**

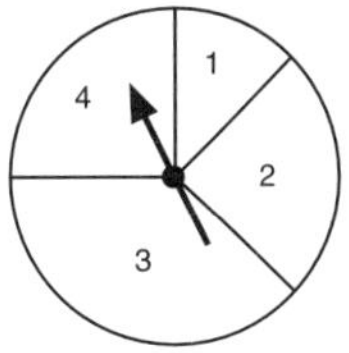


***3***



GO ON

26 **How many of the smaller figures are needed to cover the larger figure?**

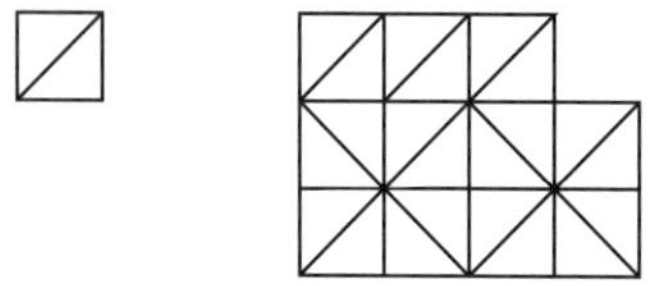

Ⓐ 22

● 11

Ⓒ 10

Ⓓ 7

27 **Which figure will have two halves that match exactly when it is folded on the solid line?**

Ⓕ 

● 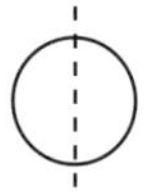

Ⓗ 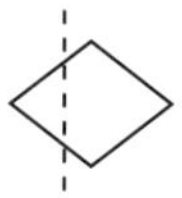

Ⓙ 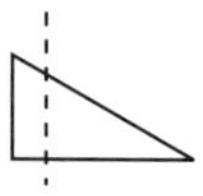

28 **Carlos drew a car on a sheet of paper.**

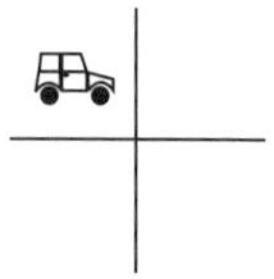

**He turns the paper so the car is in the top, right square. What does the car look like now?**

Ⓐ 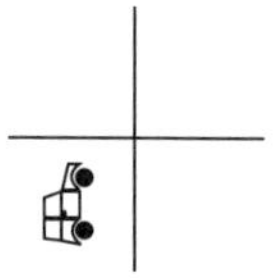

● 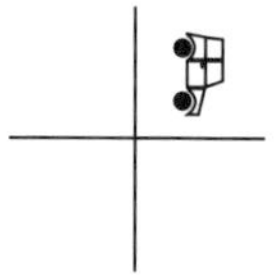

Ⓒ 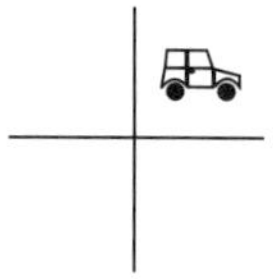

Ⓓ 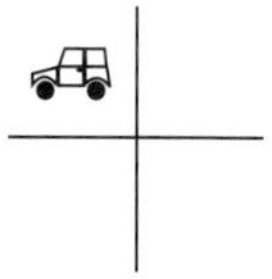



GO ON

29 **Charles found some change in his gym bag. What is the value of the money shown?**

- (F) 62¢
- ● 57¢
- (H) 27¢
- (J) 4¢

30 **About how many leaves long is the rake?**

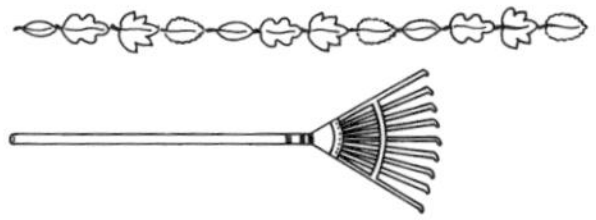

- (A) 12
- (B) 10
- ● 9
- (D) 8

31 **Which unit of measurement is best to use to describe the height of a tree?**

- (F) inches
- ● feet
- (H) pounds
- (J) miles

32 **The table below shows the number of sports cards Artie has in his collection.**

**Sports Card Collection**

| Sport | Number of Cards |
|---|---|
| Football | 16 |
| Basketball | 13 |
| Baseball | 29 |
| Soccer | 18 |
| Hockey | 9 |

**Which two categories added together equal the number of baseball cards?**

***football and basketball***

33 **The time is now 9:30. What time will it be four and one-half hours from now?**

- ● 3:00
- (B) 2:00
- (C) 1:30
- (D) 3:30

GO ON

34 **How many of the small squares are needed to fill the square shown below?**

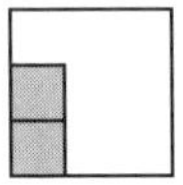

Ⓕ 7 ● 9 Ⓗ 10 Ⓙ 22

35 **The forest animals come to drink the water in a pond. Which animal lives the shortest distance from the pond?**

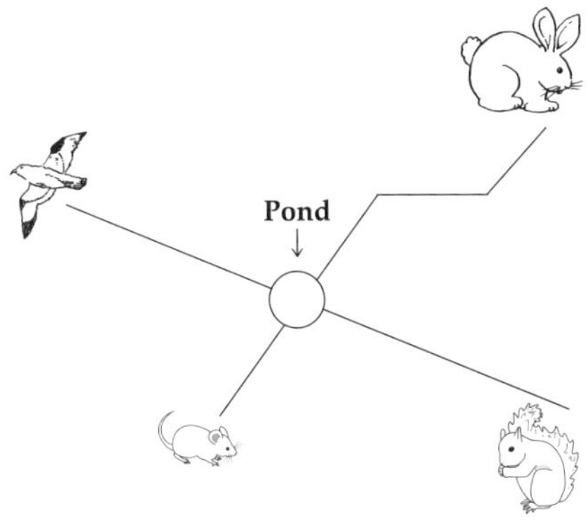

Ⓐ Ⓑ Ⓒ ●

36 **Barbara and Ronnie are raking leaves. What is the temperature like outside?**

Ⓕ 21°

Ⓖ 32°

● 55°

Ⓙ 98°

37 **Dylan bought some school supplies for $1.67. He gave the clerk $2.00. Which picture shows the coins Dylan should receive in change?**

Ⓐ

●

Ⓒ

Ⓓ



GO ON

38 **The table shows the number of animals entered in a farm show.**

| Animal | Number of Animals |
|---|---|
| Cow | 29 |
| Goats | 22 |
| Pigs | 32 |
| Sheep | 19 |

**About how many animals were entered altogether?**

● 100

Ⓖ 80

Ⓗ 70

Ⓙ 40

39 **Jared wants to buy a book for $3 and a football for $10. How much money does he need?**

Ⓐ $1

Ⓑ $5

Ⓒ $10

● $20

40 **What number is in the square, is outside the circle, and is an even number?**

Ⓕ 2

● 6

Ⓗ 9

Ⓙ 10

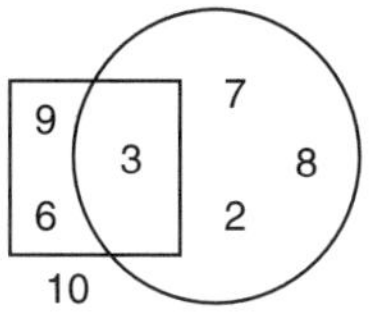


41 **Yoshi put 2 stamps on each letter she was going to mail. What do you need to know to find out how many stamps Yoshi used?**

● how many letters she was going to mail

Ⓑ how long the envelopes were

Ⓒ how many stamps she bought

Ⓓ how much the stamps cost

42 **Alice has 5 more tickets than Claire. Claire has 3 fewer tickets than Melba. Melba has 7 tickets. How many tickets does Alice have?**

Ⓕ 15

● 9

Ⓗ 6

Ⓙ 1

43 **What temperature is shown on the thermometer?**

Ⓐ 52°

● 54°

Ⓒ 58°

Ⓓ 60°

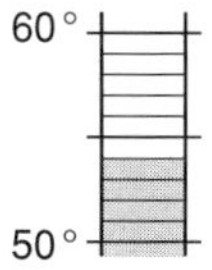


44 **Mark has 4 vases. He put 7 flowers in each vase. Write a number sentence which shows how to find the total number of flowers Mark used.**

*7 x 4 =* ☐

STOP





SAY: **It is now time to stop. You have completed the Test. Make sure that you have carefully filled in your answer spaces and have completely erased any stray marks. Then put your pencils down.**

After the test has been scored, review the questions and answer choices with students. If students are having difficulty with any lesson, provide them with additional practice items.

UNIT SEVEN

# Listening

## Listening for Word Meanings

Directions: Darken the circle for the word or words that best answer the question you hear.

**TRY THIS** Listen for key words in each sentence. Then listen carefully as each answer choice is read aloud. Decide which answer choice matches the key words and makes the most sense in the sentence.

Sample A

Ⓐ forget about it
Ⓑ guess about it
Ⓒ ignore it
● think about it

**THINK IT THROUGH** The correct answer is D, think about it. The key words in the sentence are I'd like my parents to consider. Other words that mean almost the same as consider are think about it.

STOP

1 ● goes down
Ⓑ drifts
Ⓒ expands
Ⓓ spreads out

2 Ⓕ tasty
● healthy
Ⓗ filling
Ⓙ sickening

3 ● worried
Ⓑ calm
Ⓒ thrilled
Ⓓ forgetful

4 Ⓕ very little
● extreme
Ⓗ moderate
Ⓙ limited

5 Ⓐ small
Ⓑ quick
● neat
Ⓓ tired

6 Ⓕ slowly
● quickly
Ⓗ quietly
Ⓙ heavily

7 ● glance
Ⓑ stare
Ⓒ gaze
Ⓓ observe

8 ● fee
Ⓖ allowance
Ⓗ discount
Ⓙ loan

STOP



78

# Unit 7: Listening

## Listening for Word Meanings

Reading Skill: Using definitional phrases to determine word meaning

SAY: **Turn to Listening for Word Meanings on page 78.**

Check to see that all students find page 78.

SAY: **Now you will practice choosing words or groups of words that best complete sentences.**

Read the Directions to students.

SAY: **Now look at Try This.**

Read Try This to students.

SAY: **Now look at Sample A. You will find the word that best completes the sentence. Listen carefully. I will read a sentence, followed by four answer choices. I'd like my parents to consider getting a pet. To consider something is to— A *forget about it* ...B *guess about it* ...C *ignore it* ...D *think about it.***

Allow students time to find and mark their answer. Remind students to carefully fill in the answer space and to completely erase any stray marks.

SAY: **Now look at Think It Through.**

Read Think It Through to students. Check to see that all students have filled in the correct answer space. Ask students if they have any questions.

SAY: **Now you will practice choosing more words or groups of words that best complete sentences. Now find number 1. We will do numbers 1 through 8 just as we did Sample A. Listen carefully to the sentences and the four answer choices. Then darken the circle for the correct answer.**

1 **The hot air balloon began to descend slowly. Something that descends— A *goes down* ...B *drifts* ...C *expands* ...D *spreads out.***
2 **We'll take nourishing food for the camp out. Nourishing means— F *tasty* ...G *healthy* ...H *filling* ...J *sickening.***
3 **Since I studied, I'm not anxious about the test. Anxious means—A *worried* ...B *calm* ...C *thrilled* ...D *forgetful.***

UNIT SEVEN

# Listening

## Listening for Word Meanings

Directions: Darken the circle for the word or words that best answer the question you hear.

**TRY THIS** Listen for key words in each sentence. Then listen carefully as each answer choice is read aloud. Decide which answer choice matches the key words and makes the most sense in the sentence.

**Sample A**

- Ⓐ forget about it
- Ⓑ guess about it
- Ⓒ ignore it
- ● think about it

**THINK IT THROUGH** The correct answer is D, think about it. The key words in the sentence are I'd like my parents to consider. Other words that mean almost the same as consider are think about it.

STOP

**1**
- ● goes down
- Ⓑ drifts
- Ⓒ expands
- Ⓓ spreads out

**2**
- Ⓕ tasty
- ● healthy
- Ⓗ filling
- Ⓙ sickening

**3**
- ● worried
- Ⓑ calm
- Ⓒ thrilled
- Ⓓ forgetful

**4**
- Ⓕ very little
- ● extreme
- Ⓗ moderate
- Ⓙ limited

**5**
- Ⓐ small
- Ⓑ quick
- ● neat
- Ⓓ tired

**6**
- Ⓕ slowly
- ● quickly
- Ⓗ quietly
- Ⓙ heavily

**7**
- ● glance
- Ⓑ stare
- Ⓒ gaze
- Ⓓ observe

**8**
- ● fee
- Ⓖ allowance
- Ⓗ discount
- Ⓙ loan

STOP





4 **There was intense heat coming from the blaze. Intense means— F *very little* ...G *extreme* ...H *moderate* ...J *limited.***

5 **Marco kept his toy shelf tidy. Something that is tidy is— A *small* ...B *quick* ...C *neat* ...D *tired.***

6 **The runner moved swiftly around the track. Swiftly means— F *slowly* ...G *quickly* ...H *quietly* ...J *heavily.***

7 **I only had time to glimpse the paper. To glimpse means to— A *glance* ...B *stare* ...C *gaze* ...D *observe.***

8 **We had to pay a toll to cross the bridge. A toll is a— F *fee* ...G *allowance* ...H *discount* ...J *loan.***

Allow students time to find and mark their answers.

Review the questions and answer choices with students. Discuss with the class why one answer is correct and the others are not correct. Also check to see that students have carefully filled in the answer spaces and have completely erased any stray marks.

## Building Listening Skills

Directions: Listen carefully to the story as it is read aloud. Darken the circle for the word or words that best answer the question.

**TRY THIS** Form a picture of the story in your mind. Listen carefully for details given in the story.

Sample A

- Ⓐ blow up balloons
- ● fly a kite
- Ⓒ blow whistles
- Ⓓ run a race

**THINK IT THROUGH** The correct answer is B, fly a kite. The story tells you that Josh bought a kite to fly with his big brother. He bought some balloons and whistles for his birthday party. The story does not mention running a race.

STOP

1
- Ⓐ mosquito
- Ⓑ spider
- ● butterfly
- Ⓓ lady bug

2
- Ⓕ leaves
- ● silky thread
- Ⓗ cotton
- Ⓙ twigs

3
- Ⓐ fried eggs and biscuits
- Ⓑ cheese sandwiches
- Ⓒ pancakes
- ● scrambled eggs and toast

4
- ● milk
- Ⓖ butter
- Ⓗ water
- Ⓙ bread

5
- ● today
- Ⓑ seven days ago
- Ⓒ last month
- Ⓓ two weeks ago

6
- Ⓕ smile
- Ⓖ talk
- ● eat
- Ⓙ sleep

7
- Ⓐ carrots
- Ⓑ lettuce
- ● grass
- Ⓓ cabbage

8
- Ⓕ frog
- Ⓖ rabbit
- Ⓗ little boy
- ● farmer

STOP



79

# Building Listening Skills

Reading Skill: Recalling details and sequence; drawing conclusions; making inferences; extending meaning

SAY: **Turn to Building Listening Skills on page 79.**

Check to see that all students find page 79.

SAY: **Now you will practice choosing words and phrases that best answer questions about paragraphs and stories that you hear.**

Read the Directions to students.

SAY: **Now look at Try This.**

Read Try This to students.

SAY: **Look at Sample A. I will read a story and then ask a question. You will choose the best answer to the question. Listen carefully. Josh went to the store. He bought some balloons and whistles for his birthday party next week. Then he bought a kite to fly in the park with his big brother.**

**Now look at Sample A. Listen carefully. Josh and his brother will— A *blow up balloons* …B *fly a kite* …C *blow whistles* … D *run a race.* Darken the circle for the correct answer.**

Allow students time to find and mark their answer. Remind students to carefully fill in the answer space and to completely erase any stray marks.

SAY: **Now look at Think It Through.**

Read Think It Through to students. Check to see that all students have filled in the correct answer space. Ask students if they have any questions.

SAY: **Now you will practice choosing words and phrases that best answer questions about other paragraphs and stories that you hear. Find number 1. We will do numbers 1 through 8 just as we did Sample A. Listen to the story and the question. Then darken the circle for the correct answer.**

**Now find number 1. Listen as I read this story.**

## Building Listening Skills

**Directions: Listen carefully to the story as it is read aloud. Darken the circle for the word or words that best answer the question.**

**TRY THIS** — **Form a picture of the story in your mind. Listen carefully for details given in the story.**

Sample A

- Ⓐ blow up balloons
- ● fly a kite
- Ⓒ blow whistles
- Ⓓ run a race

**THINK IT THROUGH** — **The correct answer is B, fly a kite. The story tells you that Josh bought a kite to fly with his big brother. He bought some balloons and whistles for his birthday party. The story does not mention running a race.**

STOP

1
- Ⓐ mosquito
- Ⓑ spider
- ● butterfly
- Ⓓ lady bug

2
- Ⓕ leaves
- ● silky thread
- Ⓗ cotton
- Ⓙ twigs

3
- Ⓐ fried eggs and biscuits
- Ⓑ cheese sandwiches
- Ⓒ pancakes
- ● scrambled eggs and toast

4
- ● milk
- Ⓖ butter
- Ⓗ water
- Ⓙ bread

5
- ● today
- Ⓑ seven days ago
- Ⓒ last month
- Ⓓ two weeks ago

6
- Ⓕ smile
- Ⓖ talk
- ● eat
- Ⓙ sleep

7
- Ⓐ carrots
- Ⓑ lettuce
- ● grass
- Ⓓ cabbage

8
- Ⓕ frog
- Ⓖ rabbit
- Ⓗ little boy
- ● farmer

STOP





**You will answer two questions.**

**The caterpillar makes a cocoon from a silky thread in its body. It fastens the thread to the branch of a tree and spins a cocoon around itself. There it hangs, inside the cocoon, until it turns into a butterfly. When it is ready, it breaks open the cocoon and crawls out.**

1 **The caterpillar turns into a— A *mosquito* ...B *spider* ... C *butterfly* ...D *lady bug.***

2 **The caterpillar makes its cocoon from— F *leaves* ...G *silky thread* ...H *cotton* ...J *twigs.***

**Listen as I read these directions for making breakfast. You will answer two questions about the directions.**

1. **First, take the eggs, bread, and milk out of the refrigerator.**
2. **Second, put the bread in the toaster, and toast it until it is brown.**
3. **Next, break the eggs, and use a fork to mix them with milk.**
4. **Finally, scramble the eggs in a pan on the stove.**
5. **When your breakfast is ready, enjoy!**

3 **These directions tell you how to make— A *fried eggs and biscuits* ...B *cheese sandwiches* ...C *pancakes* ... D *scrambled eggs and toast.***

4 **These directions tell you to mix the eggs with— F *milk* ... G *butter* ...H *water* ...J *bread.***

**Now find number 5. Listen as I read this story. You will answer two questions.**

**Pam has just lost her tooth. She is happy it fell out. It had been loose for seven days. Now she can eat without feeling any pain.**

5 **Pam lost her tooth—A *today* ...B *seven days ago* ...C *last month* ...D *two weeks ago.***

6 **Now it will be easier for Pam to— F *smile* ...G *talk* ...H *eat* ...J *sleep.***

**Now find number 7. Listen as I read this poem.**

## Building Listening Skills

**Directions: Listen carefully to the story as it is read aloud. Darken the circle for the word or words that best answer the question.**

**TRY THIS** Form a picture of the story in your mind. Listen carefully for details given in the story.

**Sample A**

- Ⓐ blow up balloons
- ● fly a kite
- Ⓒ blow whistles
- Ⓓ run a race

**THINK IT THROUGH** **The correct answer is B, fly a kite. The story tells you that Josh bought a kite to fly with his big brother. He bought some balloons and whistles for his birthday party. The story does not mention running a race.**

STOP

1
- Ⓐ mosquito
- Ⓑ spider
- ● butterfly
- Ⓓ lady bug

2
- Ⓕ leaves
- ● silky thread
- Ⓗ cotton
- Ⓙ twigs

3
- Ⓐ fried eggs and biscuits
- Ⓑ cheese sandwiches
- Ⓒ pancakes
- ● scrambled eggs and toast

4
- ● milk
- Ⓖ butter
- Ⓗ water
- Ⓙ bread

5
- ● today
- Ⓑ seven days ago
- Ⓒ last month
- Ⓓ two weeks ago

6
- Ⓕ smile
- Ⓖ talk
- ● eat
- Ⓙ sleep

7
- Ⓐ carrots
- Ⓑ lettuce
- ● grass
- Ⓓ cabbage

8
- Ⓕ frog
- Ⓖ rabbit
- Ⓗ little boy
- ● farmer

STOP



79

**You will answer two questions.**

**Ralph Rabbit said,**
**Oh, what a day**
**To eat cabbages and carrots and lettuce.**
**I wonder if Farmer Fred**
**Will chase us away or let us!**

7 **Ralph Rabbit did not want to eat— A *carrots* ...B *lettuce* ... C *grass* ...D *cabbage*.**

8 **Fred is a— F *frog* ...G *rabbit* ...H *little boy* ...J *farmer*.**

Review the questions and answer choices with students. Discuss with the class why one answer is correct and the others are not correct. Also check to see that students have carefully filled in the answer spaces and have completely erased any stray marks.

## Test

Sample A
- ● put in
- Ⓑ tear out
- Ⓒ plan
- Ⓓ order

STOP

1
- ● solve
- Ⓑ tie again
- Ⓒ create
- Ⓓ convince

2
- Ⓕ friendly
- ● interesting
- Ⓗ dull
- Ⓙ talkative

3
- ● tune
- Ⓑ orchestra
- Ⓒ noise
- Ⓓ singer

4
- ● careful
- Ⓖ hurried
- Ⓗ foolish
- Ⓙ important

5
- Ⓐ talk about her
- Ⓑ admire her
- ● look like her
- Ⓓ try to act like her

6
- Ⓕ common
- Ⓖ beautiful
- Ⓗ expensive
- ● unusual

7
- Ⓐ mumble
- Ⓑ laugh
- ● shout
- Ⓓ whisper

8
- Ⓕ skillful
- Ⓖ smooth
- ● awkward
- Ⓙ dangerous

9
- ● make something new
- Ⓑ find something new
- Ⓒ notice something new
- Ⓓ misplace something new

10
- Ⓕ take care of
- Ⓖ become tired of
- Ⓗ make fun of
- ● cherish

11
- Ⓐ banker
- Ⓑ teacher
- ● doctor
- Ⓓ lawyer

12
- ● careful
- Ⓖ unconcerned
- Ⓗ afraid
- Ⓙ worried



GO ON



# Test

SAY: **Turn to the Test on page 80.**

Check to see that all students find the Test.

SAY: **In this test you will use the listening skills we have practiced in this unit. This test is divided into two parts. For each part there is a sample exercise. We will work each sample together. Look at Sample A. In this part of the test, you will choose words or groups of words that best complete sentences. Listen carefully. I will read part of a sentence and four words. You will find the word that best completes the sentence. Aunt Sara is going to install new carpeting in her house. To install means to— A *put in* ...B *tear out* ...C *plan* ...D *order.* Darken the circle for the correct answer.**

Allow students time to find and mark their answer.

SAY: **You should have darkened the circle for *A, put in,* because to install is to *put in.***

Check to see that all students have filled in the correct answer space. Ask students if they have any questions.

SAY: **Now you will choose more words or groups of words that best complete sentences. Find number 1. We will do numbers 1 through 12 just as we did Sample A. Listen carefully to the sentence and the four answer choices. Then darken the circle for the correct answer.**

1. **Let's see if we can unravel this mystery. To unravel is to— A *solve* ...B *tie again* ...C *create* ...D *convince.***
2. **The author was fascinating to hear. Fascinating means— F *friendly* ...G *interesting* ...H *dull* ...J *talkative.***
3. **I can't remember where I've heard that melody before. A melody is a— A *tune* ...B *orchestra* ...C *noise* ...D *singer.***
4. **Since we didn't have much time, it was a hasty trip. Hasty means— F *careful* ...G *hurried* ...H *foolish* ...J *important.***
5. **My father resembles my grandmother. To resemble someone means to— A *talk about her* ...B *admire her* ...C *look like her* ...D *try to act like her.***

# Test

Sample A
- ● put in
- Ⓑ tear out
- Ⓒ plan
- Ⓓ order

STOP

1
- ● solve
- Ⓑ tie again
- Ⓒ create
- Ⓓ convince

2
- Ⓕ friendly
- ● interesting
- Ⓗ dull
- Ⓙ talkative

3
- ● tune
- Ⓑ orchestra
- Ⓒ noise
- Ⓓ singer

4
- ● careful
- Ⓖ hurried
- Ⓗ foolish
- Ⓙ important

5
- Ⓐ talk about her
- Ⓑ admire her
- ● look like her
- Ⓓ try to act like her

6
- Ⓕ common
- Ⓖ beautiful
- Ⓗ expensive
- ● unusual

7
- Ⓐ mumble
- Ⓑ laugh
- ● shout
- Ⓓ whisper

8
- Ⓕ skillful
- Ⓖ smooth
- ● awkward
- Ⓙ dangerous

9
- ● make something new
- Ⓑ find something new
- Ⓒ notice something new
- Ⓓ misplace something new

10
- Ⓕ take care of
- Ⓖ become tired of
- Ⓗ make fun of
- ● cherish

11
- Ⓐ banker
- Ⓑ teacher
- ● doctor
- Ⓓ lawyer

12
- ● careful
- Ⓖ unconcerned
- Ⓗ afraid
- Ⓙ worried



GO ON



6 **This old book is extremely rare. Rare means— F *common* ...G *beautiful* ...H *expensive* ...J *unusual.***

7 **Mom asked us not to speak very loudly in the house. To speak very loudly is to— A *mumble* ...B *laugh* ...C *shout* ...D *whisper.***

8 **The new puppy was clumsy as he tried to chase us. Clumsy means— F *skillful* ...G *smooth* ...H *awkward* ... J *dangerous.***

9 **Maya wants to invent a machine to help pick up toys. To invent is to— A *make something new* ...B *find something new* ...C *notice something new* ...D *misplace something new.***

10 **Jamal and his family adore his new baby brother. To adore means to— F *take care of* ...G *become tired of* ...H *make fun of* ...J *cherish.***

11 **Jeff visits his physician at least once every year. A physician is a— A *banker* ...B *teacher* ...C *doctor* ... D *lawyer.***

12 **We were cautious when crossing the street. Cautious means— F *careful* ...G *unconcerned* ...H *afraid* ...J *worried.***

**Sample B**

Ⓐ park
Ⓑ museum
Ⓒ store
● library

STOP

**13**
● play
Ⓑ costume
Ⓒ mask
Ⓓ race

**14**
Ⓕ dragon
Ⓖ evil queen
● prince
Ⓙ princess

**15**
● raincoat
Ⓑ winter coat
Ⓒ sweater
Ⓓ dress

**16**
Ⓕ "A Rainy Day"
Ⓖ "Fun at Summer Camp"
Ⓗ "The Best Breakfast"
● "Carmela's Problem"

**17**
Ⓐ loving
● foolish
Ⓒ sad
Ⓓ afraid

**18**
Ⓕ washes the dishes
● makes her bed
Ⓗ walks the dog
Ⓙ does her homework

**19**
● Gloria washes the dishes.
Ⓑ Gloria takes out the trash.
Ⓒ Gloria makes her bed.
Ⓓ Gloria helps her mother cook.

**20**
● the kite can fly
Ⓖ the kite won't blow away
Ⓗ you can decorate the kite
Ⓙ you can catch the kite

**21**
Ⓐ tin
● cloth
Ⓒ paper
Ⓓ wood

**22**
Ⓕ throw away more trash
Ⓖ learn how to pollute
● pick up trash
Ⓙ do not be concerned about it

**23**
Ⓐ bottles
● pollution
Ⓒ newspapers
Ⓓ cans

STOP





SAY: **Now turn to page 81. Look at Sample B.**

Check to see that all students find Sample B on page 81.

SAY: **In this part of the test, you will choose words and phrases that best answer questions about paragraphs and stories that you hear. I will read a story and then ask a question. You will choose the best answer to the question. Listen carefully. Mike's mom took him and his little brother to the library. They saw some of their friends there. Together they watched a puppet show. Mike and his brother had a great time.**

**Now look at Sample B. Listen carefully. Mike and his family went to the— A *park* ...B *museum* ...C *store* ...D *library.* Darken the circle for the correct answer.**

Allow students time to find and mark their answer.

SAY: **You should have darkened the circle for *D*, *library,* because the first sentence of the story says that Mike's mom took Mike and his little brother to the *library*.**

Check to see that all students have filled in the correct answer space. Ask students if they have any questions.

SAY: **Now you will choose more words and phrases that best answer questions. We will do numbers 13 through 23 just as we did Sample B. Listen carefully to the story and question. Then darken the circle for the correct answer.**

**Now find number 13. Listen carefully as I read this story. You will answer two questions.**

> **Miss Matay's class put on a play. Cara played a princess. Lori played an evil queen who was jealous of the princess. Tony played a prince who comes to save the princess. "You have the best part in the play," Miss Matay told Vinnie. "You get to play the part of the dragon."**

13 **Miss Matay's class put on a— A *play* ...B *costume* ... C *mask* ...D *race.***

14 **Tony played the part of the—F *dragon* ...G *evil queen* ... H *prince* ...J *princess.***

**Now find number 15. Listen as I read this story. You will answer two questions.**

**Mr. Hernandez packed Carmela's suitcase for summer camp. He packed her play clothes, pajamas, robe, and a swimsuit. On the morning of the second day at camp, it rained very hard. Carmela got ready to walk to the camp kitchen for breakfast. She then discovered that her father had forgotten to pack something.**

15 **Mr. Hernandez forgot to pack Carmela's— A *raincoat* ... B *winter coat* ...C *sweater* ...D *dress.***

16 **Which of these would be the best title for this passage? F *"A Rainy Day"* ...G *"Fun at Summer Camp"* ...H *"The Best Breakfast"* ...J *"Carmela's Problem."***

**Now find number 17. Listen as I read this poem. You will answer one question.**

**"Silly me," said Samantha Stocks,**
**"How did I do this?"**
**Her cat jumped out of her lunch box!**

17 **Samantha probably felt— A *loving* ...B *foolish* ...C *sad* ... D *afraid.***

**Now find number 18. Listen as I read this story. You will answer two questions.**

**Gloria helps her mother with the housework every day. Before going to school, Gloria makes her bed. After school, she does her homework. Then she helps her mother cook. She takes out the trash. Finally, she washes the dishes after dinner.**

18 **Before she goes to school, Gloria— F *washes the dishes* ...G *makes her bed* ...H *walks the dog* ...J *does her homework.***

19 **How does Gloria help her mother after dinner? A *Gloria washes the dishes* ....B *Gloria takes out the trash* .... C *Gloria makes her bed* ....D *Gloria helps her mother cook.***

**Now find number 20. Listen as I read these directions. You will answer three questions.**

1. **First, take the kite out of the package.**
2. **Second, insert the wooden pieces into the back of the kite.**
3. **Next, attach the end of a ball of string to the center of the kite.**
4. **Finally, make a kite's tail from pieces of cloth and attach it to the kite.**
5. **If you'd like, you can paint or decorate your kite.**

20 **The reason wooden pieces are attached to the kite is so that— F *the kite can fly* ...G *the kite won't blow away* ... H *you can decorate the kite* ...J *you can catch the kite.***

21 **According to the directions, the kite's tail can be made from pieces of— A *tin* ...B *cloth* ...C *paper* ...D *wood.***

**Now find number 22. Listen carefully as I read this story. You will answer two questions.**

**Many people are concerned about the environment. There are a number of things that you can do to help clean up the environment. You can pick up trash. You can collect and recycle newspapers, cans, and bottles. You can learn about what causes pollution. Of course, it is easier and more fun to do these things with other people.**

22 **One way to protect the environment is to— F *throw away more trash* ...G *learn how to pollute* ...H *pick up trash* ... J *do not be concerned about it.***

23 **One of the things that cannot be recycled is— A *bottles* ... B *pollution* ...C *newspapers* ...D *cans.***

SAY: **It is now time to stop. You have completed the Unit 6 Test. Make sure you have carefully filled in your answer spaces and have completely erased any stray marks. Then put your pencils down.**

After the test has been scored, review the questions and answer choices with students. If students are having difficulty with any lesson, provide them with additional practice.

UNIT EIGHT

# Language

## Prewriting, Composing, and Editing

**Directions: Darken the circle for the correct answer to each question, or write in the answer.**

**TRY THIS**

**Pretend that you are writing each sentence. Use the rules you have learned for capitalization, punctuation, and writing clear, correct sentences.**

### Rosalina's Trip

Rosalina and her family went to Canada on vacation. They went to many places and had a great time. Rosalina wanted to tell her friend about her trip. So she wrote her a letter.

**Sample A**

Dear Debbie,
I want to tell you about the great time I had **(1)** in Canada. We visited many places. **(2)** I liked **(3)** visiting Niagara Falls the best. My friend had **(4)** a great time in Hawaii

**Which sentence does not belong in Rosalina's letter?**

- Ⓐ 1
- Ⓑ 2
- Ⓒ 3
- ● 4

**THINK IT THROUGH**

**The correct answer is D, 4. This sentence does not tell about the topic of the paragraph, which is a vacation in Canada.**

STOP

**Here is the next part of Rosalina's letter.**

In Ontario, canada, we visited the **(5)** Welland Ship Canal. We watched a **(6)** huge ship travel through the canal.

**1** **Write Ontario, canada correctly.**

***Ontario, Canada***

STOP





# Unit 8: Language

## Prewriting, Composing, and Editing

Language Skills: Identifying appropriate sources of information; using parts of a book to locate information; understanding dictionary entries; determining topic relevance; alphabetizing words; determining appropriate topic sentences and supporting sentences; identifying extraneous information within a paragraph; distinguishing between clearly written sentences and sentences that contain errors in expression and construction; identifying correctly applied grammar; identifying correct capitalization and punctuation; identifying correctly and effectively written sentences

SAY: **Turn to Prewriting, Composing, and Editing on page 82.**

Check to see that all students find page 82.

SAY: **Now you will practice various language skills.**

Read the Directions to students.

SAY: **Now look at Try This.**

Read Try This to students.

SAY: **Read the information in the box entitled, "Rosalina's Trip." Now look at Sample A. Read the part of the letter silently. Then read the question and answer choices carefully. Darken the circle for the correct answer.**

Allow students time to find and mark their answer.

UNIT EIGHT

# Language

## Prewriting, Composing, and Editing

**Directions: Darken the circle for the correct answer to each question, or write in the answer.**

**TRY THIS** **Pretend that you are writing each sentence. Use the rules you have learned for capitalization, punctuation, and writing clear, correct sentences.**

### Rosalina's Trip

Rosalina and her family went to Canada on vacation. They went to many places and had a great time. Rosalina wanted to tell her friend about her trip. So she wrote her a letter.

**Sample A**

Dear Debbie,
I want to tell you about the great time I had (1) in Canada. We visited many places. (2) I liked visiting Niagara Falls the best. (3) My friend had a great time in Hawaii (4)

**Which sentence does not belong in Rosalina's letter?**

Ⓐ 1
Ⓑ 2
Ⓒ 3
● 4

**THINK IT THROUGH** **The correct answer is D, 4. This sentence does not tell about the topic of the paragraph, which is a vacation in Canada.**

STOP

**Here is the next part of Rosalina's letter.**
In Ontario, canada, we visited the (5) Welland Ship Canal. We watched a (6) huge ship travel through the canal.

1 **Write Ontario, canada correctly.**

***Ontario, Canada***

STOP





SAY: **Now look at Think It Through.**

Read Think It Through to students. Check to see that all students have filled in the correct answer space. Ask students if they have any questions.

SAY: **Now you will practice using your language skills as you read more sentences and paragraphs. Read each set of directions and each paragraph carefully. Then do numbers 1 through 25 just as we did Sample A. If no choices are given, write in your answer. When you come to the arrow with the words *GO ON* at the bottom of a page, continue working on the next page. When you come to the stop sign at the bottom of page 88, put your pencils down. You may now begin.**

Allow students time to find and mark their answers.

## The Whale

Alfred's teacher wanted the students in the class to write a report about their favorite animal. Alfred's favorite animal is the whale. So Alfred decided to write his paper about the whale.

**2 Alfred put these words in alphabetical *(ABC)* order so he could find them more quickly in the dictionary. Which list is correct?**

- Ⓐ flippers–flukes–fins–fat
- Ⓑ fat–flukes–fins–flippers
- ● fat–fins–flippers–flukes
- Ⓓ fins–fat–flippers–flukes

**3 If Alfred wanted to find the meaning of the word *fluke*, where should he look first?**

- ● a dictionary
- Ⓖ an encyclopedia
- Ⓗ an atlas
- Ⓙ a language arts book

**4 Where could Alfred probably find the most information about whales?**

- Ⓐ a newspaper
- ● an encyclopedia
- Ⓒ a dictionary
- Ⓓ a language arts book



**Alfred found the book *The Whale* in the library. Use the Table of Contents from this book to answer questions 5–7.**

### Table of Contents



**5 Information about what whales eat begins on page—**

***4***

**6 In which chapter can Alfred find information about the way whales speak to one another?**

| 3 | 4 | 5 | 6 |
|---|---|---|---|
| Ⓕ | Ⓖ | Ⓗ | ● |

**7 Alfred can find information about the food that whales eat in Chapter—**

| 2 | 3 | 4 | 6 |
|---|---|---|---|
| Ⓐ | Ⓑ | ● | Ⓓ |

GO ON

**Here is the first part of Alfred's report. Read it carefully. Then answer questions 8–11.**

## The Whale

It was easy to choose my favorite animal. It is the whale.
**(1)** **(2)**
Jerry's favorite animal is the tiger. Did you know that whales did
**(3)** **(4)**
not always live in the ocean? Millions of years ago, whales were
**(5)**
land animals. Walked around on four legs. They lived near the
**(6)** **(7)**
oceans. They hunted in the waters near the shore. In time, the
**(8)** **(9)**
whales went deeper into the sea. They began to feel more at
**(10)**
home in the ocean than on land. They became whales as we
**(11)**
know them today.



8 **Which group of words is not a complete sentence? Write the number of the group of words.**

*6*

9 **What is the best way to write sentence 5?**

- Ⓕ The whales millions of years ago were land animals.
- Ⓖ The whales were millions of years ago land animals.
- Ⓗ Land animals were whales millions of years ago.
- ● As it is written.

10 **Which sentence does not belong in Alfred's report?**

| 1 | 3 | 5 | 7 |
|---|---|---|---|
| Ⓐ | ● | Ⓒ | Ⓓ |

11 **What is the best way to combine sentences 7 and 8 without changing their meaning?**

- Ⓕ Living near the ocean, they hunted in waters near the shore.
- ● They lived near the oceans and hunted in the waters near the shore.
- Ⓗ They hunted near the shore and lived near the ocean.
- Ⓙ They lived and hunted near the waters by the oceans.

No part of this document may be reproduced without the written permission of the publisher.

GO ON

Here is the next part of Alfred's report. This part has groups of words underlined. Read this part carefully. Then answer questions 12–15.

> Whales can be found in all the oceans of the world! Some
> (12) (13)
> whales live in water so deep that they are almost never seen.
>
> Other whales live close to shore, so they're seen often. Most
> (14) (15)
> whales travels from place to place. They moves during
> (16)
> different times of the year. Whales feed in the cold waters
> (17)
> near the North and South Poles for part of the year. Ther'es
> (18)
> much more food for whales there than in warmer waters.
>
> Whales travel to warmer waters to have their babies.
> (19)



**12 In sentence 12, oceans of the world! is best written—**

- Ⓐ oceans of the world?
- ● oceans of the world.
- Ⓒ oceans of the world,
- Ⓓ As it is written.

**13 In sentence 15, Most whales travels is best written—**

- ● Most whales travel
- Ⓖ Most whales traveling
- Ⓗ Most whales traveled
- Ⓙ As it is written.

**14 In sentence 16, They moves during different times is best written—**

- Ⓐ They moved during different times
- Ⓑ They move'd during different times
- ● They move during different times
- Ⓓ As it is written.

**15 In sentence 18, Ther'es much more food is best written—**

- Ⓕ Theres' much more food
- ● There's much more food
- Ⓗ The'res much more food
- Ⓙ As it is written.

GO ON

### Time to go Camping!

Millie and her family go camping every summer. This year they will go with Millie's cousin Tara and her family. Millie decides to write Tara a letter to help her get ready for camping.

16 **If Millie wanted to learn more about how to write a letter, she should look in—**

- ● a language arts book.
- Ⓑ a dictionary.
- Ⓒ an atlas.
- Ⓓ an encyclopedia.

**Millie made a list of things that Tara should bring for camping. Use her list to answer question 17.**

### Supplies For Camping

1. a tent
2. a warm sleeping bag
3. a flashlight
4. food for three days
5. plates, cups, spoons, forks, and knives
6. some snacks
7.

17 **Which of these is not something Millie should list as number 7?**

- Ⓕ marshmallows to roast
- ● nice jewelry to wear
- Ⓗ a bucket to put out a campfire
- Ⓙ a cooler to keep food cold

**While Millie was writing her letter, she needed to check some words in the dictionary.**

18 **What definition best fits the word trail as used in the sentence below? Write the definition.**

**We went for a walk on the trail.**

***a path or track***

GO ON

Here is the first page of Millie's letter. Read the letter carefully. Then answer questions 19–21.

Dear Tara,

I'm so glad that you will be able to go camping with us. I
**(1)** **(2)**
can't wait! I know that you have never gone camping. So I
**(3)** **(4)**
want to tell you about it. Going camping is so much fun. You'll
**(5)** **(6)**
get to be outside for three whole days. You'll get to eat outside.
**(7)**
We'll cook food on a stove. We'll cook over a fire. At night you
**(8)** **(9)** **(10)**
can see thousands of stars in the sky. Sleeping in a tent is also
**(11)**
a lot of fun. All the cousins will be able to sleep in the same tent.
**(12)**

**19** **What is the best way to combine sentences 8 and 9 without changing their meaning?**

Ⓐ We'll cook food on a stove, we'll cook over a fire.

Ⓑ On a stove and over a fire we'll cook food.

Ⓒ On a stove we'll cook food and over a fire we'll cook food.

● We'll cook food on a stove and over a fire.

**20** **What is the topic sentence of this paragraph?**

*5*

**21** **What is the best way to write sentence 12?**

Ⓕ In the same tent all the cousins will get to sleep.

Ⓖ All the cousins in the same tent will get to sleep.

Ⓗ All the cousins. Will get to sleep in the same tent.

● As it is written.

GO ON

Here is the next part of Millie's letter. This part has groups of words underlined. Read this part carefully. Then answer questions 22–25.

You need to get things ready for camping. Your parents will
(13) (14)
bring the tent. You should bring an warm sleeping bag. You
(15) (16)
should also bring a flashlight. It's so much fun to use flashlights
(17)
to walk around the camp at night. Make sure you bring pots
(18)
pans, and dishes. You'll need them to cook your food. Hot dogs
(19) (20)
and hamburgers taste great when you're camping! Make sure
(21)
you brought a lot of marshmallows. We'll be roasting them over
(22)
the fire. I'm also going to bring some fruit and some granola bars.
(23)
You should bring some, too.
(24)

sincerely yours,
Millie

**22 In sentence 15, bring an warm sleeping bag is best written—**

- Ⓐ brought an warm sleeping bag
- ● bring a warm sleeping bag
- Ⓒ brought a warm sleeping bag
- Ⓓ As it is written

**23 In sentence 18, bring pots pans, and dishes is best written—**

- ● bring pots, pans, and dishes
- Ⓖ bring pots pans and dishes
- Ⓗ bring pots, pans and dishes
- Ⓙ As it is written

**24 In sentence 21, brought a lot of is best written—**

- Ⓐ brings a lot of
- Ⓑ bringing a lot of
- ● bring a lot of
- Ⓓ As it is written

**25 At the end of Millie's letter, sincerely yours, is best written—**

- Ⓕ Sincerely Yours,
- ● Sincerely yours,
- Ⓗ sincerely Yours,
- Ⓙ As it is written

STOP





Review the questions and answer choices with students. Discuss with the class why one answer is correct and the others are not correct. Also check to see that students have carefully filled in the answer spaces and have completely erased any stray marks.

## Identifying Misspelled Words

Directions: Read each sentence carefully. If one of the words is misspelled, darken the circle for that word. If all the words are spelled correctly, then darken the circle for *No Mistake*.

**TRY THIS** Read each sentence carefully. If you are not sure of an answer, first decide which answer choices are spelled correctly. Then see if you can recognize the misspelled word from your reading experience.

Sample A

May played a livly tune on her piano. No mistake

● Ⓑ Ⓒ Ⓓ

**THINK IT THROUGH** The correct answer is A, for the first underlined word. All of the other words are spelled correctly. Livly should be spelled l-i-v-e-l-y. You should not drop the e when you add -ly.

STOP

1 In sewing class I am making an aperun for my mom. No mistake

Ⓐ Ⓑ ● Ⓓ

2 We saw some unusual butterflies in the woods. No mistake

Ⓕ Ⓖ Ⓗ ●

3 Don told the scaryest ghost story at camp. No mistake

● Ⓑ Ⓒ Ⓓ

4 The car startd to slide on the icy highway. No mistake

● Ⓖ Ⓗ Ⓙ

5 The magical king granted the shoemaker three wishs. No mistake

Ⓐ Ⓑ ● Ⓓ

STOP





# Identifying Misspelled Words

Language Skills: Demonstrating the ability to identify misspellings of words in the context of sentences; identifying correct spellings of words

SAY: **Turn to Identifying Misspelled Words on page 89.**

Check to see that all students find page 89.

SAY: **Now you will identify misspelled words and words that are spelled correctly.**

Read the Directions to students.

SAY: **Now look at Try This.**

Read Try This to students.

SAY: **Now look at Sample A. Read the sentence carefully. If one of the words is misspelled, darken the circle for that word. If all the words are spelled correctly, darken the circle for *No mistake*.**

Allow students time to find and mark their answer.

SAY: **Now look at Think It Through.**

Read Think It Through to students. Check to see that all students have filled in the correct answer space. Ask students if they have any questions.

SAY: **Now you will practice identifying more misspelled words and words that are spelled correctly. Do numbers 1 through 5 just as we did Sample A. When you come to the stop sign at the bottom of the page, put your pencils down. You may now begin.**

Allow students time to find and mark their answers.

Review the questions and answer choices with students. Discuss with the class why one answer is correct and the others are not correct. Also check to see that students have carefully filled in the answer spaces and have completely erased any stray marks.

## Test

Sample A

**Go Fly a Kite**

Leon's scout troop has entered a kite contest. Leon knows how to make and fly a kite. He wants to write a paper to help the other scouts get ready for the contest.

**Leon wants to find out when the kite contest in his city will take place. He should look in—**

Ⓐ an atlas.

Ⓑ an encyclopedia.

Ⓒ a dictionary.

● a newspaper.

STOP

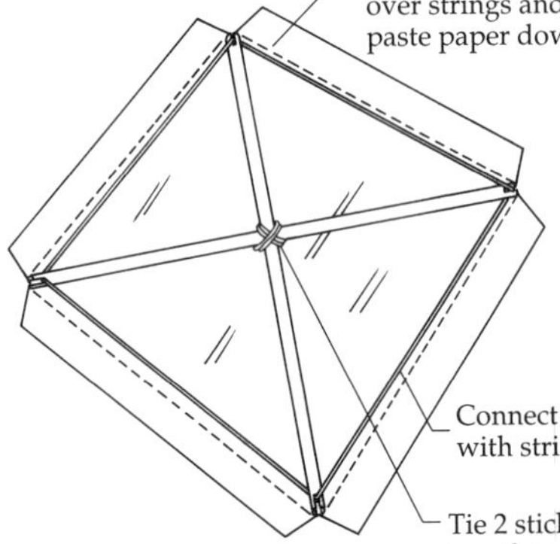


1 **Here is a sketch Leon drew of a kite. How will it best help him to write his paper?**

Ⓐ It will help him picture what kind of paper to use.

● It will help him picture how to put the kite together.

Ⓒ It will help him remember a kite contest he once entered.

Ⓓ It will help him decide to enter the kite contest.

2 **Leon found the book *How To Fly a Kite*. Where in the book should he look to find the author's name?**

Ⓕ Chapter 1

● the title page

Ⓗ the table of contents

Ⓙ the index

3 **If Leon wanted to find out when kites were first made, where should he look?**

Ⓐ a dictionary

Ⓑ an atlas

Ⓒ a language arts book

● an encyclopedia

4 **Where should Leon look to find the meaning of the word fasten?**

***a dictionary***



GO ON



# Test

SAY: **Turn to the Test on page 90.**

Check to see that all students find the Test.

SAY: **In this test you will use the language skills that we have practiced in this unit. Look at Sample A. Read the paragraph entitled "Go Fly a Kite" carefully. Then read the question and the answer choices. Darken the circle for the correct answer.**

Allow students time to find and mark their answer.

SAY: **You should have darkened the circle for *D*, next to *a newspaper*, because a newspaper would be the best place to look to find out when a current event was going to take place.**

Check to see that all students have filled in the correct answer space. Ask students if they have any questions.

SAY: **Now you will finish the test on your own. Do numbers 1 through 24 just as we did Sample A. Read each set of directions and each paragraph carefully. Then read the questions and answer choices carefully. Darken the circle for each correct answer, or write in the answer. For questions 25 through 32, darken the circle for the word that is misspelled. If all the words are spelled correctly, darken the circle for *No mistake*. When you come to the arrow with the words *GO ON* at the bottom of a page, continue working on the next page. When you come to the stop sign at the bottom of page 96, put your pencils down. You may now begin.**

Allow students time to find and mark their answers.

**Here is the first part of Leon's paper. Read it carefully. Then answer questions 5–7.**

## How to Make a Kite

I'm going to tell you how to make a flat kite. Make sure that
(1) (2)
you have two sticks, string, paper, and glue. Take the two sticks
(3)
and cross them into an *X*. Use the string to tie the sticks together.
(4)
Tie them tightly where the two sticks cross. Then add glue to make
(5) (6)
sure the two sticks stay together. Around the ends of the sticks tie
(7)
a string. This will be the outer edge of the kite. Then cut a large
(8) (9)
piece of paper. Fold the edges of the paper over the string all
(10)
around the kite. Use paste to glue the paper around the string.
(11)
My sister made a beautiful kite.
(12)

**5 What is the topic sentence of this paragraph?**

| 1 | 2 | 3 | 4 |
|---|---|---|---|
| ● | Ⓖ | Ⓗ | Ⓙ |

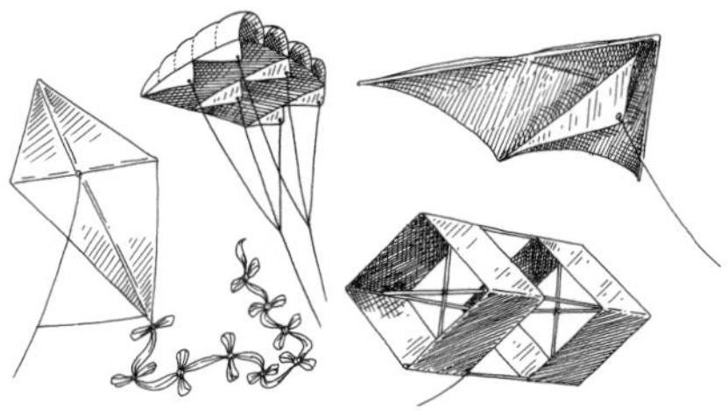

**6 What is the best way to write sentence 7?**

- Ⓐ Around the ends of the sticks a string tie.
- ● Tie a string around the ends of the sticks.
- Ⓒ A string tie around the ends of the sticks.
- Ⓓ As it is written.

**7 Which sentence does not belong in Leon's paper? Write the number.**

*12*

GO ON

**Here is the next part of Leon's paper. This part has groups of words underlined. Read this part carefully. Then answer questions 8–11.**

The Kite Contest will take place in April. The most important
**(13)** **(14)**
thing to remember is that your kite has to fly. Then you can enter
**(15)**
your kite in three events. The first event will decide which kite is
**(16)**
decorated the best. The judges will look at the colors and designs
**(17)**
you use. The second event will decide which kite can fly the
**(18)**
highest. The judges will give you about ten minutes to get your
**(19)**
kite into the air! The third event will decide how fast you can
**(20)**
send out your kite to the end of the line and reels it in again.

Lets' all get busy and get our kites ready!
**(21)**

**8 In sentence 13, The Kite Contest is best written—**

- ● The kite contest
- Ⓖ The Kite contest
- Ⓗ the kite Contest
- Ⓙ As it is written.

**9 In sentence 19, into the air! is best written—**

- Ⓐ into the air?
- Ⓑ into the air,
- ● into the air.
- Ⓓ As it is written.

**10 In sentence 20, and reels it in again. is best written—**

- ● and reel it in again.
- Ⓖ and reeling it in again.
- Ⓗ and reel's it in again.
- Ⓙ As it is written.

**11 In sentence 21, Lets' all get is best written—**

- Ⓐ Lets all get
- ● Let's all get
- Ⓒ Le'ts all get
- Ⓓ As it is written.



GO ON

## Learning About the Moon

Mary and her class went on a field trip to a planetarium. Her teacher wanted each student to write a paper and tell about one thing they learned. Mary decided to write about the moon.

**12 Why is Mary writing the paper?**

Ⓕ to tell about the moon and planets

Ⓖ to ask her parents to go to the planetarium

Ⓗ to describe the moon

● to tell what she learned at the planetarium

**13 Mary put these words in alphabetical *(ABC)* order so she could find them more quickly in the dictionary. Which list is correct?**

● meteors – moonrise – motion – mountains

Ⓑ moonrise – mountains – meteors – motion

Ⓒ mountains – motion – moonrise – meteors

Ⓓ meteors – motion – moonrise – mountains



**Mary found the book *The Moon* in the library. Use the Table of Contents and Index from the book to answer questions 14–16.**

### Table of Contents

| Chapter | | Page |
|---|---|---|
| 1 | How the Moon Looks | 5 |
| 2 | How the Moon Came To Be | 22 |
| 3 | What Holds the Moon in the Sky? | 29 |
| 4 | How Hot Is It on the Moon? | 36 |
| 5 | People Who Have Explored the Moon | 43 |

### Index

craters, 7–8
gravity, 25
moon
 age of, 23–24
 distance from Earth, 29
space program, 43–45

**14 In which chapter could Mary find information about the astronauts who walked on the moon?**

| 2 | 3 | 4 | 5 |
|---|---|---|---|
| Ⓕ | Ⓖ | Ⓗ | ● |

**15 Mary can find information about moon craters on page—**

| 8 | 23 | 25 | 43 |
|---|---|---|---|
| ● | Ⓑ | Ⓒ | Ⓓ |

**16 Information about how the moon came to be can be found in Chapter—**

***2***

GO ON

**Here is the first part of Mary's report. Read it carefully. Then answer questions 17–20.**

## Learning About the Moon

I really enjoyed going to the planetarium. **(1)** I learned a lot about the moon. **(2)** The moon is smaller than Earth. **(3)** Jupiter is the largest planet. **(4)** The moon is about 238,000 miles away from Earth. **(5)** That's not very far when you're talking about outer space. **(6)** You cannot live on the moon. **(7)** The moon has no water. **(8)** It has no air. **(9)** During the day the moon is hot. **(10)** Enough to fry an egg. **(11)** At night, the moon is colder than the North Pole. **(12)** The moon is covered with dust–covered flat land. **(13)** It also has many different sizes of craters. **(14)**

**17 Which of these is not a complete sentence?**

| 5 | 7 | 9 | 11 |
|---|---|---|---|
| Ⓕ | Ⓖ | Ⓗ | ● |

**18 What is the best way to combine sentences 8 and 9 without changing their meaning?**

- Ⓐ The moon, which has no air, has no water.
- Ⓑ The moon has no water and the moon has no air.
- ● The moon has no water and no air.
- Ⓓ The moon having no water has no air.

**19 Which sentence does not belong in Mary's paper?**

| 2 | 4 | 6 | 8 |
|---|---|---|---|
| Ⓕ | ● | Ⓗ | Ⓙ |

**20 Which of these could be added after sentence 14?**

- ● Some of the craters are old volcanoes.
- Ⓑ Some planets have more than one moon.
- Ⓒ Jamie liked visiting the planetarium, too.
- Ⓓ Earth is the third planet from the sun.



GO ON

Here is the next part of Mary's report. This part has groups of words underlined. Read this part carefully. Then answer questions 21–24.

I really liked learning about the people who explored the moon.
**(15)**
The first people walked on the moon on July 20, 1969? They
**(16)** **(17)**
take a walk that lasted more than two hours. They gathered
**(18)**
rocks and soil to bring back to Earth to study. They also took
**(19)**
many photographs. Before they left for Earth these people set
**(20)**
up experiments on the moon. More people walk on the moon
**(21)**
after 1969. Some of them rode in a special kind of car called
**(22)**
a lunar rover. The work of these people
**(23)**
helped us learn a lot about the moon.

**21** **In sentence 16, on July 20, 1969? is best written—**

- Ⓕ on July 20, 1969,
- ● on July 20, 1969.
- Ⓗ On July 20, 1969?
- Ⓙ As it is written.

**22** **In sentence 17, They take a walk is best written—**

- Ⓐ They taking a walk
- Ⓑ They takes a walk
- ● They took a walk
- Ⓓ As it is written.

**23** **In sentence 21, More people walk is best written—**

- ● More people walked
- Ⓖ More people is walking
- Ⓗ More people walks
- Ⓙ As it is written.

**24** **In sentence 23, these people helped us is best written—**

- Ⓐ these people helping us
- Ⓑ these people is helped us
- Ⓒ these people has helping us
- ● As it is written.

GO ON

For questions 25–32, read each sentence carefully. If one of the words is misspelled, darken the circle for that word. If all the words are spelled correctly, then darken the circle for *No mistake.*

25 Ashley was very lonly in the cabin by the lake. No mistake

● Ⓖ Ⓗ Ⓙ

26 Nick dashd down the street to catch the bus. No mistake

● Ⓑ Ⓒ Ⓓ

27 Flashs of light streaked across the sky during the storm. No mistake

● Ⓖ Ⓗ Ⓙ

28 The plane flew through the clowds. No mistake

Ⓐ Ⓑ ● Ⓓ

29 The kitten raced into the alley when the dog barked. No mistake

Ⓕ Ⓖ Ⓗ ●

30 Bob walked to the store to buy vegetables. No mistake

Ⓐ Ⓑ Ⓒ ●

31 Phil enjoys reading advenchure stories. No mistake

Ⓕ ● Ⓗ Ⓙ

32 This is the greasyest pan I've ever washed! No mistake

● Ⓑ Ⓒ Ⓓ



STOP



SAY: **It is now time to stop. You have completed the Test. Make sure that you have carefully filled in your answer spaces and have completely erased any stray marks. Then put your pencils down.**

After the test has been scored, review the questions and answer choices with students. If students are having difficulty with any lesson, provide them with additional practice items.

UNIT NINE

# Practice Test 1

## Reading Comprehension

Sample A

### Cathy's Vacation Plans

Cathy is excited about going camping with her family this summer. They plan to go to the Grand Canyon where they will stay for two weeks.

**How long will Cathy's family camp?**

Ⓐ two days

● two weeks

Ⓒ two months

Ⓓ the entire summer

STOP

**For questions 1–32, read each story and the questions that follow. Then darken the circle for the correct answer to each question, or write in the answer.**

### How to Plant a Tree

Planting a tree is a good way to clean the air, provide a home for birds, and make the world more beautiful. You will need a tree, a shovel, and *mulch.*

First, choose a good spot for the tree. It should not be too close to a building or other trees or beneath telephone wires. Dig a two-foot-deep hole with sloping sides.

Second, remove or cut away the container that the tree is in. Pick up the tree by the root ball, not the trunk, and set it in the hole. Then fill the hole with dirt around the root ball. When the hole is a little more than half full, fill the hole with water and stir the mud with your shovel. This will settle the soil and remove air pockets. Then finish filling in the hole with dirt.

Last, place *mulch,* or leaves, straw or bark, around the tree. Water the tree and step back to admire your work!

1 **Planting a tree will do all of the following except—**

Ⓐ make the world more beautiful.

● save water.

Ⓒ clean the air.

Ⓓ provide a home for birds.

2 **What can be used to make mulch?**

***leaves, straw, or bark***

GO ON





# Comprehensive Tests

## Practice Test 1: Reading Comprehension

Allow 30 minutes for this test.

SAY: **Turn to Practice Test 1, Reading Comprehension, on page 97.**

Check to see that all students find Practice Test 1.

SAY: **In this test you will use your reading skills to answer questions about stories that you read. Look at Sample A. Read the story silently. Then answer the question that follows. *How long will Cathy's family camp?* A *Two days* ...B *Two weeks* ...C *Two months* ... D *The entire summer.* Darken the circle for the correct answer.**

Allow students time to find and mark their answer.

SAY: **You should have darkened the circle for *B, Two weeks,* because the selection states that Cathy's family will go to the Grand Canyon for two weeks.**

Check to see that all students have filled in the correct answer space. Ask students if they have any questions.

SAY: **Now you will finish the test on your own. Do questions 1 through 32 just as we did Sample A. Read each selection carefully. Then darken the circle for the correct answer, or write in your answer. When you come to the arrow with words *GO ON* at the bottom of a page, continue working on the next page. When you come to the stop sign at the bottom of page 104, put your pencils down. You have 30 minutes to complete the test. You may now begin.**

Allow students 30 minutes to find and mark their answers.

## When Grandma Was a Young Girl

Grandma has told me many stories about what it was like growing up on the farm when she was a girl. Her family lived ten miles from any neighbors. They had little money to buy food in a store. They had to grow most of their food on the farm. They raised cows and chickens for meat. They grew and then canned fruits and vegetables to last the whole winter. Grandma's family stored some of the food in an underground cellar to keep it from spoiling. They also had an underground spring near the house. The water was very cold. They stored milk, butter, and eggs in the spring to keep them fresh.

Grandma and her family had to work very hard. I am glad that we have cars and can go to the grocery store to buy our food.

3 **The writer thinks that Grandma's life on the farm was—**

- ● difficult.
- Ⓖ easy.
- Ⓗ fun.
- Ⓙ boring.

4 **How did the family keep milk and butter fresh?**

- Ⓐ They canned it.
- ● They stored it in a spring.
- Ⓒ They used a refrigerator.
- Ⓓ They kept it in a cellar.

5 **Why did Grandma's family have to grow most of their food?**

***There was little money to buy food in a store.***

6 **Which question does the first paragraph answer?**

- Ⓕ How big was the farm?
- Ⓖ What was the grandmother's favorite thing to do?
- ● How did the family get food?
- Ⓙ Where did the grandmother go to school?



GO ON

## All About Bees

Bees are always busy. Worker bees fly from flower to flower, and then they fly back to the beehive. There the worker bees make honey. They help the queen bee by building nests. They also clean the nests and take care of baby bees. The queen bee lays all the eggs for the beehive. The work that bees do is useful to people. Bees help plants grow in gardens and on farms. The sweet honey that bees make is delicious to eat.

**7 Worker bees do all of the following except—**

Ⓐ make honey.

● lay eggs.

Ⓒ clean the nest.

Ⓓ take care of baby bees.

**8 What job does the queen bee have?**

***laying eggs***

**9 What is another good title for this story?**

● "Busy, Busy Bees"

Ⓖ "How Honey is Made"

Ⓗ "A Day in the Life of a Queen Bee"

Ⓙ "Why Bees Like Flowers"

**10 How is the work that bees do useful to people?**

Ⓐ Bees clean their own nests.

● Bees help plants grow in gardens and on farms.

Ⓒ Bees are fun to watch.

Ⓓ Bees are always busy.

GO ON

## An Important Food

When you think of bread, what comes to mind? Do you think of a fresh loaf of white bread? Perhaps you picture a nice loaf of wheat bread. If you lived in another country, you might have a very different idea of bread. A boy or girl in Mexico would think of *tortillas*. These are flat, round breads made from corn. People in India would think of *chappatis*. These are heavy pieces of round bread that are fried.

Bread is one of the most important foods. It is eaten more than any other food. It is also eaten in more places than any other food.

Bread has been an important food for a very long time. The first bread was made about 12,000 years ago. People in the Middle East gathered the seeds of wild plants. They used the seeds to make flour. They mixed the flour with water. Then they baked it on hot rocks.

Later people learned how to plant seeds so they could grow their own wheat. People in Egypt learned that if they added yeast to the flour and water, it would make the bread rise. The Egyptians also learned to build ovens in which to bake the bread.

For hundreds of years, bread was made in the same way. But in time, people wanted a light bread. They learned that if flour was sifted through cloth, the rough pieces could be taken out. Then they would have white flour. From white flour, soft white bread could be made. For many years only rich people could buy white bread. Today many people like whole-wheat bread better than white bread. We know that the rough pieces of flour are good for us.

GO ON

11 **You would probably find this story in a book called—**

- ● *Important Foods Around the World.*
- Ⓖ *Holidays in Many Places.*
- Ⓗ *Foods from Mexico.*
- Ⓙ *How to Grow Wheat.*

12 **Who first added yeast to bread?**

- ● Egyptians
- Ⓑ people in the Middle East
- Ⓒ Germans
- Ⓓ Mexicans

13 **What question does the second paragraph answer?**

- Ⓕ How is bread made?
- ● What food is eaten more than any other?
- Ⓗ Who made the first bread?
- Ⓙ What kind of bread do people like best?

14 **To answer question 11, the reader should—**

- Ⓐ reread the first line of each paragraph.
- Ⓑ reread the last paragraph of the story.
- ● look for the word *chappatis* in the story.
- Ⓓ reread the title of the story.

15 **What is this story mainly about?**

- Ⓕ how to make bread
- Ⓖ how to eat bread
- Ⓗ types of flat bread
- ● the history of bread

16 **If the story continued, it would probably tell about—**

- ● ways bread is made today.
- Ⓑ how to eat a healthful diet.
- Ⓒ medicines made from plants.
- Ⓓ favorite foods of children.

17 **What are *chappatis*?**

- Ⓕ flat, round breads made of corn
- Ⓖ sweet biscuits
- ● heavy pieces of fried bread
- Ⓙ soft, rye breads

18 **What was bread first made from?**

***the seeds from wild plants***



GO ON

## Visiting Grandmother

Tino loves to visit his grandmother. He doesn't get to visit her very often because his family lives in a city that is six hours away. His grandmother lives in a big wooden house on a farm. It is old and looks like it has secret hiding places.

On the second Sunday of July, Tino's parents took him to his grandmother's. Since it was summer vacation, he was going to stay at Grandmother's for a whole month! His cousins Doug and Barbara would soon be arriving. They would also be staying at their grandmother's this summer.

A big porch wraps around two sides of the house. Tino sat in the porch swing. He could see the trees that circle the house. They had been planted as a *windbreak.* They protect the house from the wind and blowing dirt. The house is in the middle of a large, flat field.

Tino watched the dirt road that leads to the house. He couldn't wait for his cousins to get there! Doug was his age, and Barbara was a year younger. They always had fun together. Last summer they had spent one whole morning making a fort out of sacks of seed that they found in the barn. Then Uncle John had taken them on a tractor ride.

Tino remembered another time with his cousins. They had gone out to explore the fields. Tino touched an electric fence and got a shock. Then they found an old snakeskin. Nothing like that ever happened at home! Tino took the snakeskin to school and showed it to everyone.

Tino could smell the dinner that his mother and grandmother were cooking. He smelled ham, hot rolls, and pumpkin pie. It made him hungry.

Finally he saw a cloud of dust coming up the road. "They're here! They're here!" he shouted.

GO ON

19 **After Tino's cousins arrive, what will probably happen next?**

Ⓐ They will build a fort on the hill.

Ⓑ They will look for snakeskins.

Ⓒ They will climb the trees in their grandmother's yard.

● They will eat dinner at their grandmother's house.

20 **In order to answer question 21, the reader should—**

Ⓕ read the title of the story again.

Ⓖ read the first paragraph again.

● look in the story for the word *windbreak*.

Ⓙ read the last line of each paragraph again.

21 **How do you think Tino felt when he saw his cousins arriving?**

Ⓐ He was worried.

● He was excited.

Ⓒ He was angry.

Ⓓ He was sad.

22 **Tino's grandmother lives in a—**

Ⓕ brick house.

Ⓖ stone house.

● wooden house.

Ⓙ new house.

23 **What is meant by a *windbreak?***

***trees that protect a house from the wind***

24 **The story tells about Tino and his cousins doing all of the following except—**

● watching old movies.

Ⓑ taking a tractor ride.

Ⓒ finding a snakeskin.

Ⓓ making a fort from seed sacks.

25 **Tino's grandmother's house was—**

Ⓕ on a hill.

Ⓖ in a valley.

● in a field.

Ⓙ in a city.

26 **These boxes show events that happened in the story.**

| 1 | 2 | 3 |
|---|---|---|
| Tino went to Grandmother's house. | | Tino thought about another visit to Grandmother's. |

**What belongs in box 2?**

Ⓐ Tino's cousins arrived at Grandmother's house.

Ⓑ Tino could smell dinner cooking.

● Tino sat in the porch swing.

Ⓓ Tino saw a cloud of dust coming up the road.



GO ON

This poster was placed in the cafeteria at Taft Elementary School.

**Help Our Environment!**

April is "Help Our Environment!" month at Taft Elementary School. Students can help clean up our planet by collecting used cans, bottles, and newspapers. These things should be put in the recycling bins that have been placed in each classroom. Each class that fills its bin will get a "Clean Class" award. On Earth Day each student in these classes will get to plant a tree in the schoolyard. Let's all help make our school and our world a cleaner place!

**27 According to the poster, all of the following activities will happen in April except—**

- Ⓕ collecting cans, bottles, and newspapers.
- Ⓖ filling recycling bins.
- Ⓗ planting trees.
- ● taking a trip to the recycling center.

**28 What will probably happen after the recycling bins are filled?**

- ● The materials will be taken to a recycling center.
- Ⓑ The materials will be sent home with students.
- Ⓒ The materials will be stored at the school.
- Ⓓ The materials will be buried in the schoolyard.

**29 Where was this sign posted?**

- Ⓕ at the neighborhood gym
- ● at Taft Elementary School
- Ⓗ at the supermarket
- Ⓙ at East High School

**30 The recycling bins are for—**

- Ⓐ bottles and cans.
- Ⓑ bottles, plastic, and newspapers.
- Ⓒ cans, plastic, and cardboard.
- ● cans, bottles, and newspapers.

**31 Who will get to plant trees?**

- ● classes who get a "Clean Class" award
- Ⓖ students who buy a tree
- Ⓗ students who read the most books
- Ⓙ classes who make the best grades

**32 When will the "Help Our Environment" program be held?**

***during the month of April***



STOP



SAY: **It is now time to stop. You have completed Test 1. Make sure that you have carefully filled in your answer spaces and have completely erased any stray marks. Then put your pencils down and close your books.**

After the test has been scored, review the questions and answer choices with students. If students are having difficulty, provide them with additional practice.

UNIT TEN

# Practice Test 2

## Reading Vocabulary

Sample A

**A parka is a kind of—**

● warm jacket with a hood
Ⓑ European folk dance
Ⓒ dried meat
Ⓓ sled

STOP

**For questions 1-9, darken the circle for the word or words that have the same or almost the same meaning as the underlined word.**

1 **Familiar means—**

Ⓐ old
Ⓑ beautiful
● known
Ⓓ strange

2 **A lane is most like a—**

Ⓕ ladder
● road
Ⓗ shack
Ⓙ race

3 **To cure means to—**

● heal
Ⓑ clean
Ⓒ study
Ⓓ correct

4 **A tourist is a kind of—**

Ⓕ judge
Ⓖ chair
Ⓗ teacher
● visitor

5 **To recall something is to—**

Ⓐ prepare it
Ⓑ clean it
● remember it
Ⓓ include it

6 **Something that is precise is—**

Ⓕ expensive
● exact
Ⓗ rare
Ⓙ safe

7 **Something that is soaked is—**

● wet
Ⓑ dirty
Ⓒ soiled
Ⓓ wrinkled

8 **A jacket is most like a—**

Ⓕ hat
Ⓖ dress
● coat
Ⓙ jar

9 **A kennel is a place for—**

● dogs
Ⓑ airplanes
Ⓒ plants
Ⓓ cars

STOP

105



# Practice Test 2: Reading Vocabulary

Allow 15 minutes for this test.

SAY: **Turn to Practice Test 2 on page 105.**

Check to see that all students find Practice Test 2.

SAY: **In this test you will use your reading skills to answer questions. This test is divided into three parts. For each part there is a sample exercise. We will work each sample together. In the first part of the test, you will find words that mean the same or almost the same as the underlined word. Now look at Sample A. Read the sentence and the answer choices. A *parka* is a kind of—*warm jacket with a hood...European fold dance...dried meat...sled.* Darken the circle for the word that has the same or almost the same meaning as the underlined word, *parka.***

Allow students time to find and mark their answer.

SAY: **You should have darkened the circle for *A, warm jacket with a hood. Warm jacket with a hood* is closest in meaning to the underlined word, *parka.***

Check to see that all students have filled in the correct answer space.
Ask students if they have any questions.

SAY: **Now you will finish this part of the test on your own. Read the directions carefully. Do numbers 1 through 9 just as we did Sample A. Darken the circle for each correct answer. When you come to the stop sign at the bottom of page 105, put your pencils down. You may now begin.**

Allow students time to find and mark their answers.

Sample B

Turn the key to make the car run.

In which sentence does run have the same meaning as it does in the sentence above?

- Ⓐ Water will always run downhill.
- ● This fan won't run any more.
- Ⓒ Li will run in the race today.
- Ⓓ I hit a run at our baseball game.

STOP

For questions 10–14, darken the circle for the sentence in which the underlined word means the same as it does in the sentence in the box.

10 Draw a card and put it on the table.

In which sentence does draw have the same meaning as it does in the sentence above?

- Ⓕ We used horses to draw the wagon.
- Ⓖ Please draw a picture of a whale for me.
- Ⓗ The circus will draw a big crowd.
- ● Each of us will draw a number from the hat.

11 We saw a boat sail on the bay.

In which sentence does bay have the same meaning as it does in the sentence above?

- Ⓐ The wolf began to bay at the moon.
- Ⓑ The winner was the bay horse.
- ● The water in that bay is icy.
- Ⓓ Put a bay leaf in the soup.

12 I ate part of the pie.

In which sentence does part have the same meaning as it does in the sentence above?

- Ⓕ I won't part with my favorite jacket.
- ● Joe did part of the work.
- Ⓗ Trevor played the part of Peter Pan.
- Ⓙ The part in your hair is crooked.

13 Always check your answers.

In which sentence does check have the same meaning as it does in the sentence above?

- Ⓐ Dad wrote a check for the clothes.
- Ⓑ I put a check beside my name.
- Ⓒ My marker is on the red check.
- ● Check to see if you have your ticket.

14 We took a lunch break at noon.

In which sentence does break have the same meaning as it does in the sentence above?

- Ⓕ That old chain may break.
- Ⓖ At this ranch they break horses.
- ● If you are tired, take a break.
- Ⓙ The sun shone through a break in the clouds.



STOP



SAY: **Now turn to page 106. Find Sample B.**

Check to see that all students find Sample B on page 106.

SAY: **In this part of the test, you will match words that have more than one meaning. Look at Sample B. Read the sentence in the box and the question below it. Always check your answers. In which sentence does *run* have the same meaning as it does in the sentence above? *Water will always run downhill... This fan won't run anymore...Li will run in the race today... I hit a run at our baseball game.* Darken the circle for the sentence that uses the word *run* in the same way as the sentence in the box.**

Allow students time to find and mark their answer.

SAY: **You should have darkened the circle for *B*. In that sentence, *run* means "to work," just as it does in the sentence in the box.**

Check to see that all students have filled in the correct answer space. Ask students if they have any questions.

SAY: **Now you will finish this part of the test on your own. Read the directions carefully. Do numbers 10 through 14 just as we did Sample B. Darken the circle for each correct answer. When you come to the stop sign at the bottom of page 106, put your pencils down. You may now begin.**

Allow students time to find and mark their answers.

Sample C

That delicate fruit will bruise easily if it is bumped. Bruise means—

● mark

Ⓑ hurt

Ⓒ blossom

Ⓓ taste

STOP

For questions 15–21, darken the circle for the word or words that give the meaning of the underlined word, or write in the answer.

15 He tried to navigate the space shuttle safely through the asteroid field. Navigate means—

Ⓐ dock

Ⓑ chase

Ⓒ land

● steer

16 We were astounded by the magician's amazing tricks. Astounded means—

*amazed*

17 That organization works to preserve and protect the environment. Preserve means—

Ⓕ clean up

Ⓖ plant flowers

Ⓗ hunt animals

● keep from being lost

18 He was in a hurry and had time for only a brief visit. Brief means—

Ⓐ afternoon

● short

Ⓒ casual

Ⓓ lunch

19 He didn't want to lie so he gave him an honest answer. Honest means—

● truthful

Ⓖ false

Ⓗ strange

Ⓙ long

20 She inscribed his name on the clay vase with a sharp pen. Inscribed means—

● wrote

Ⓑ burned

Ⓒ read

Ⓓ underlined

21 If you plan to attend the party, please send a reply. Reply means—

● answer

Ⓖ car

Ⓗ invitation

Ⓙ cake

STOP

107



SAY: **Now turn to page 107. Find Sample C.**

Check to see that all students find Sample C on page 107.

SAY: **In this part of the test, you will use clue words to help you figure out the meaning of the underlined word. Look at Sample C. Read the sentence and the four answer choices. That delicate fruit will bruise easily if it is bumped. Bruise means—*mark...hurt...blossom...taste.* Darken the circle for the word that has the same or almost the same meaning as the underlined word, *bruise.***

Allow students time to find and mark their answer.

SAY: **You should have darkened the circle for *A*, *mark,* because *bruise* means the same as *mark.***

Check to see that all students have filled in the correct answer space. Ask students if they have any questions.

SAY: **Now you will finish this part of the test on your own. Read the directions carefully. Do numbers 15 through 21 just as we did Sample C. Darken the circle for each correct answer, or write in your answer. When you come to the stop sign at the bottom of page 107, put your pencils down. You may now begin.**

Allow students time to find and mark their answers.

SAY: **It is now time to stop. You have finished Practice Test 2. Make sure that you have carefully filled in your answer spaces and have completely erased any stray marks. Then put your pencil down.**

After the test has been scored, review the questions and answer choices with students. If students are having difficulty, provide them with additional practice.

UNIT ELEVEN

# Practice Test 3

## Part 1: Math Problem Solving

**Sample A**

**Which is another way to write 700 + 10 + 5?**

Ⓐ 700,105 Ⓒ 7,150

Ⓑ 7,001 ● 715

STOP

**For questions 1–43, darken the circle for the correct answer, or write in the answer.**

1 **Which number belongs on the number line at point C?**

Ⓐ 42 ● 48

Ⓑ 47 Ⓓ 51

2 **Jean has an even number of stamps in her stamp collection. Which is Jean's stamp collection?**

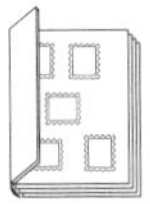

Ⓕ 45

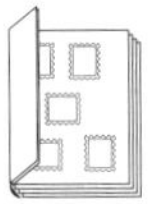

Ⓗ 51

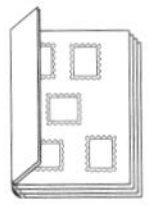

Ⓖ 49

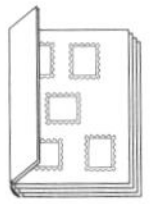

● 52

3 **Which number has a 5 in the hundreds place?**

Ⓐ 5,640 Ⓒ 56

● 564 Ⓓ 5

4 **The table shows the number of people who go to the movies during the week.**

| Day | Number of People |
|---|---|
| Monday | 243 |
| Tuesday | 146 |
| Wednesday | 297 |
| Thursday | 185 |
| Friday | 324 |

**On which day did the fewest number of people go to the movies?**

Ⓕ Monday Ⓗ Thursday

● Tuesday Ⓙ Friday

5 **Which is another name for two thousand one hundred sixty?**

Ⓐ 216 ● 2,160

Ⓑ 2,106 Ⓓ 21,600

6 **The chart shows the number of students in grades one through four.**

| One | Two | Three | Four |
|---|---|---|---|
| 290 | 163 | 249 | 312 |

**Which of the following shows the grades listed in order from the fewest number of students to the most students?**

● Two, three, one, four

Ⓖ Three, two, one, four

Ⓗ Four, two, one, three

Ⓙ One, two, three, four



GO ON



# Practice Test 3

## Part 1: Math Problem Solving

Allow about 50 minutes for this test.

Distribute scratch paper to students. Tell them they may use the scratch paper to work the problems.

Distribute inch and centimeter rulers to students or make sure they have these rulers. Tell them they may use the rulers to solve some problems.

SAY: **Turn to Practice Test 3 on page 108.**

Check to see that all students find Practice Test 3.

SAY: **In this test you will use your mathematics skills to solve problems. Look at Sample A. Which is another way to write 700 + 10 + 5? Look at the answer choices carefully. Then darken the circle for the correct answer.**

Allow students time to choose and mark their answer.

SAY: **You should have darkened the circle for *D, 715*. Another way to write 700 + 10 + 5 is 715.**

Check to see that all students have filled in the correct answer space. Ask students if they have any questions.

SAY: **Now you will finish the test on your own. Read the directions carefully. Then read each question and the answer choices carefully. Darken the circle for the correct answer, or write in your answer. Do numbers 1 through 43 just as we did Sample A. When you come to the arrow and the words *GO ON* at the bottom of a page, continue working on the next page. When you come to the bottom of page 114, put your pencils down. You have 50 minutes to complete the test. You may now begin.**

Allow students 50 minutes to find and mark their answers.

7 **Which number sentence is in the same fact family as**

| 9 − 6 = 3 | ?

● 6 + 3 = 9

Ⓑ 9 + 6 = 15

Ⓒ 6 − 3 = 3

Ⓓ 6 ≥ 3 = 18

8 **Which number belongs in the box to make the number sentence correct?**

**2 × □ = 9 × 2**

Ⓕ 2 Ⓗ 11

● 9 Ⓙ 18

9 **Which is another way to write 4 × 2?**

Ⓐ 2 × 2 × 2 × 2

Ⓑ 8 + 2

Ⓒ 4 + 2

● 2 + 2 + 2 +2

10 **Which number belongs in the box to make the number sentence correct?**

**5 × □ = 5**

Ⓕ 10 ● 1

Ⓖ 5 Ⓙ 0

11 **What fraction of the shape is not shaded?**

$\frac{1}{5}$

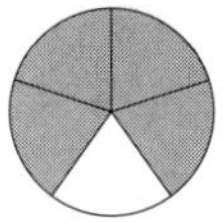

12 **Which picture shows $\frac{2}{3}$ of the flowers shaded?**

Ⓐ  ● 

Ⓑ  Ⓓ 

13 **The pizza restaurant cuts each pizza into 6 slices. What is the missing number that completes the pattern in the chart?**

| Pizzas | Number of Slices |
|---|---|
| 1 | 6 |
| 2 | ? |
| 3 | 18 |
| 4 | 24 |

Ⓕ 1 Ⓗ 7

Ⓖ 6 ● 12

14 **The students in Mrs. James' class must collect 20 leaves. The table shows the fraction of leaves each student has collected so far.**

| Name | Fraction Collected |
|---|---|
| Ken | $\frac{1}{4}$ |
| Dominic | $\frac{1}{5}$ |
| Jenna | $\frac{1}{10}$ |
| Perry | $\frac{1}{2}$ |

**Which student collected the smallest fraction of leaves?**

Ⓐ Ken ● Jenna

Ⓑ Dominic Ⓓ Perry

GO ON

The graph below shows the kinds of sports stories students in Ms. Kent's class wrote. Study the graph and answer questions 15 and 16.

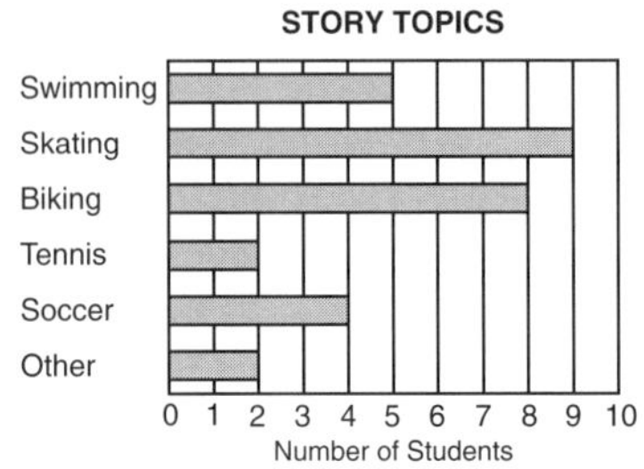


**15** **How many students wrote about skating?**

***9***

**16** **How many more students wrote about skating than soccer?**

● 5    Ⓗ 9

Ⓖ 7    Ⓙ 13

**17** **The tally chart shows the number of butterflies 4 students spotted during a week.**

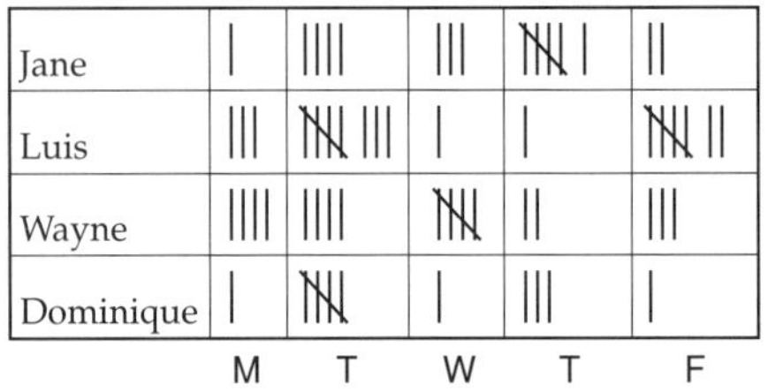


**Who spotted more than 5 butterflies but fewer than 10 on Tuesday?**

Ⓐ Jane    Ⓒ Wayne

● Luis    Ⓓ Dominique

**18** **The chart below shows the number of ounces in cartons of juice.**

| Juice | Ounces |
|---|---|
| Orange | 5.3 |
| Apple | 5.6 |
| Grape | 6.1 |
| Cranberry | 4.5 |

**Which juice carton has the most ounces?**

Ⓕ Orange    ● Grape

Ⓖ Apple    Ⓙ Cranberry

**19** **What is the missing number that completes the pattern in the boxes?**

| | | | | |
|---|---|---|---|---|
| **3** | **9** | **15** | **21** | |

Ⓐ 23    ● 27

Ⓑ 25    Ⓓ 30

**20** **Which shows the piece missing from the figure?**

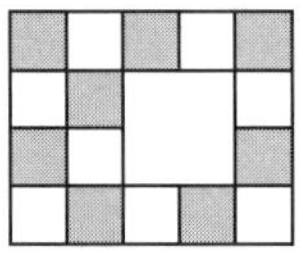

Ⓕ

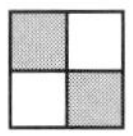

Ⓗ

Ⓖ

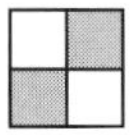

●



GO ON

21 **Which names the location of [rocket]?**

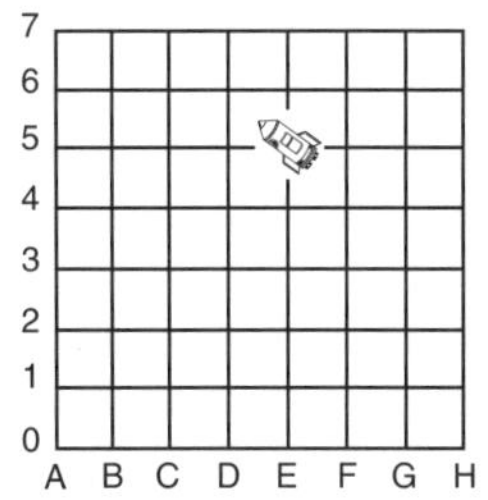


Ⓐ G3 ● E5

Ⓑ F4 Ⓓ D6

22 **Florence is playing a game with the spinner. Which month will the next spin least likely show?**

***May***

23 **The table below shows the number of books students in Mrs. Wallin's class have read.**

| Name | Number of Books |
|---|---|
| Marilyn | 18 |
| Penny | 27 |
| Lillian | 15 |
| Kyle | 30 |
| Jim | 29 |

**Who read 14 more books than Lillian?**

● Jim Ⓗ Penny

Ⓖ Kyle Ⓙ Marilyn

24 **Look at the numbered shapes. Which two figures are exactly the same in size and shape?**

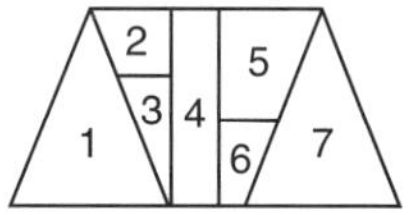


Ⓐ 2 and 5 Ⓒ 3 and 6

● 1 and 7 Ⓓ 1 and 4

25 **What shape does the can have?**

● cylinder

Ⓖ cube

Ⓗ cone

Ⓙ sphere

26 **These shapes were picked from a bag.**

**If one more shape is picked from the bag, which of these shapes will it most likely be?**

Ⓐ 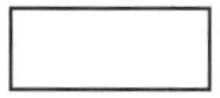 ● 

Ⓑ 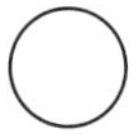 Ⓓ 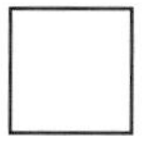

GO ON

27 **Which shape has four corners and four sides that are exactly the same length?**

Ⓕ 

● 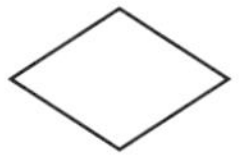

Ⓗ 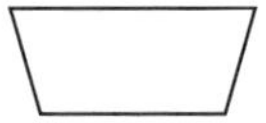

Ⓙ 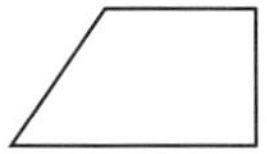

28 **Clara made a card for her mother.**

**She turns the card so the words are on the bottom. What does the card look like now?**

Ⓐ 

Ⓑ 

Ⓒ 

● 

29 **Carmen gets home from school at 3:30. She leaves for baseball practice one and one-half hours later. What time will it be when Carmen leaves for baseball practice?**

Ⓕ 8:00

● 5:00

Ⓗ 3:00

Ⓙ 12:00

30 **Which unit of measurement is best to use to measure the weight of an apple?**

Ⓐ pounds

Ⓑ inches

Ⓒ quarts

● ounces

31 **Which figure will have two halves that match exactly when it is folded on the solid line?**

● 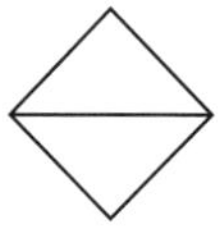

Ⓗ 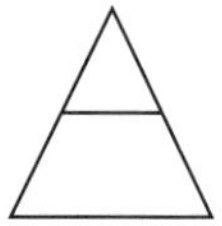

Ⓖ 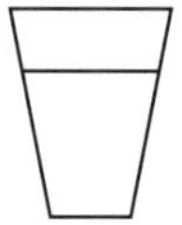

Ⓙ 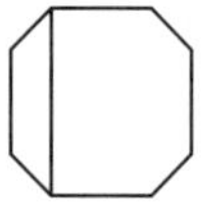



GO ON

**32** **Carmine bought a football helmet that cost $9.84. He gave the store clerk $10.00. Which coins should Carmine receive in change?**

● 

Ⓑ 

Ⓒ 

Ⓓ 

**33** **Aris found these coins in his yard. What is the value of the money shown?**

Ⓕ 36¢ ● 50¢

Ⓖ 41¢ Ⓙ 61¢

**34** **What temperature is shown on the thermometer?**

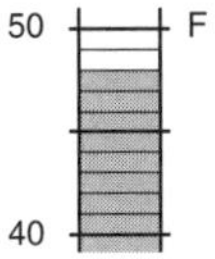


Ⓐ 41°

● 48°

Ⓒ 52°

Ⓓ 90°

**35** **How many inches long is the trail from where the squirrel is to the nuts? Use your inch ruler to answer this question.**

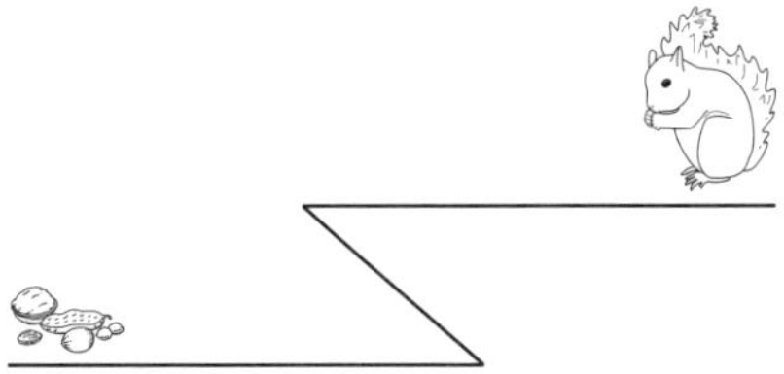

Ⓕ 3 inches Ⓗ 7 inches

● 5 inches Ⓙ 9 inches

**36** **A bird is building a nest. The lines show how far it flies to get the grass and twigs for the nest. Which line shows the longest distance the bird flies from the nest?**

Ⓐ 1

Ⓑ 2

Ⓒ 3

● 4

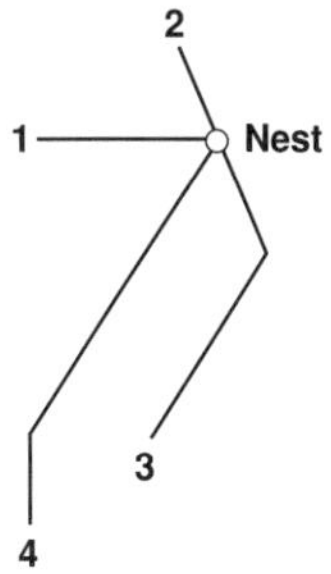


**37** **How many of the small squares are needed to fill the rectangle?**

Ⓕ 25

Ⓖ 20

● 15

Ⓙ 3

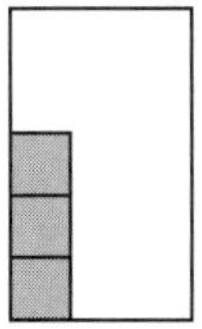

GO ON

38 Crystal is 5 years younger than Carlos. Carlos is 3 years younger than Don. Don is 13. How old is Crystal?

Ⓐ 16 ● 5

Ⓑ 10 Ⓓ 1

39 The table shows how the third-grade students at Main Street Elementary travel to school.

| Way of Travel | Number of Students |
|---|---|
| Car | 38 |
| Bus | 73 |
| Bicycle | 9 |
| Walk | 9 |

About how many third-grade students are there altogether?

Ⓕ 80 ● 130

Ⓖ 100 Ⓙ 140

40 About how much did Chip spend on 2 shirts and a jacket?

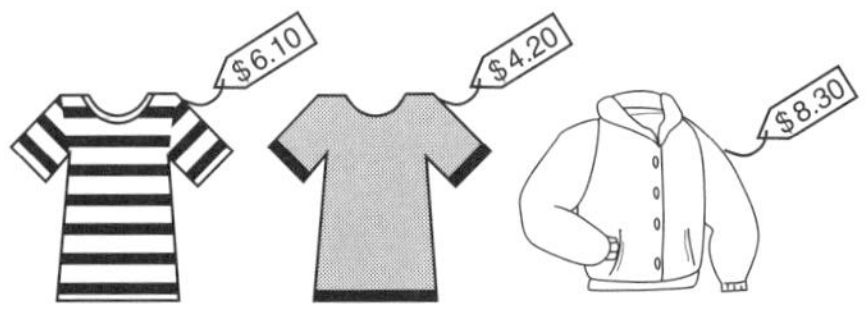


Ⓐ $10 Ⓒ $30

● $20 Ⓓ $40

41 What number is inside the circle, is outside the square, and is an even number?

Ⓕ 11

● 12

Ⓗ 13

Ⓙ 15

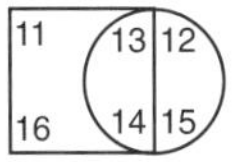


42 Mr. Takata put the top of his car down before going for a drive. What is the temperature outside like?

● 87°

Ⓑ 41°

Ⓒ 32°

Ⓓ 15°

43 Dawn sold 15 calendars on Thursday. She sold 30 on Sunday. Which number sentence shows how to find the total number of calendars Dawn sold?

● 30 + 15 = □

Ⓖ 30 − 15 = □

Ⓗ □ + 15 = 30

Ⓙ 30 × 15 = □



GO ON



SAY: **It is now time to stop. You have completed Part 1 of Practice Test 3. Make sure you have carefully filled in your answer spaces and have completely erased any stray marks. Then put your pencils down.**

After the test has been scored, review the questions and answer choices with students. If students are having difficulty, provide them with additional practice.

## Part 2: Math Procedures

Sample A

5 × 7 = □

| 35 | 30 | 25 | 20 | NH |
|---|---|---|---|---|
| ● | Ⓑ | Ⓒ | Ⓓ | Ⓔ |

STOP

**For questions 1–22, darken the circle for the correct answer. If the correct answer is not here, darken the circle for NH. If no choices are given, write in the answer.**

**1**

$$\begin{array}{r} 711 \\ 28 \\ +\ 84 \end{array}$$

| 713 | 722 | 823 | 1831 | NH |
|---|---|---|---|---|
| Ⓐ | Ⓑ | ● | Ⓓ | Ⓔ |

**2**

$$\begin{array}{r} 324 \\ -\ 228 \end{array}$$

| 94 | 97 | 104 | 106 | NH |
|---|---|---|---|---|
| Ⓕ | Ⓖ | Ⓗ | Ⓙ | ● |

**3**

7 + □ = 14

| 9 | 8 | 7 | 6 | NH |
|---|---|---|---|---|
| Ⓐ | Ⓑ | ● | Ⓓ | Ⓔ |

**4**

$$\begin{array}{r} 8 \\ \times\ 8 \end{array}$$

| 16 | 56 | 64 | 72 | NH |
|---|---|---|---|---|
| Ⓕ | Ⓖ | ● | Ⓙ | Ⓚ |

**5**

$$\begin{array}{r} 95 \\ -\ 16 \end{array}$$

| 111 | 101 | 89 | 79 | NH |
|---|---|---|---|---|
| Ⓐ | Ⓑ | Ⓒ | ● | Ⓔ |

**6**

$$\begin{array}{r} 625 \\ +\ 39 \end{array}$$

| 654 | 664 | 754 | 764 | NH |
|---|---|---|---|---|
| Ⓕ | ● | Ⓗ | Ⓙ | Ⓚ |

**7**

$$\begin{array}{r} 648 \\ -\ 63 \end{array}$$

***585***

**8**

$$\begin{array}{r} 46 \\ +\ 27 \end{array}$$

***73***

GO ON





# Part 2: Math Procedures

Allow about 25 minutes for this test.

Distribute scratch paper to students. Tell them they may use the scratch paper to work the problems.

SAY: **Turn to Part 2 of the Practice Test on page 115.**

Check to see that all students find page 115.

SAY: **In this test you will use your mathematics skills to solve computation and word problems. Now look at Sample A. You are asked to find the answer to 5 x 7. Work the problem. Then darken the circle for the correct answer. If the correct answer is not given, darken the circle for *NH, not here.***

Allow students time to find and mark their answer.

SAY: **You should have darkened the circle for *A, 35,* because *5 x 7 = 35.***

SAY: **Now look at Sample B on page 117. Roberto bought 11 pencils. Each pencil cost 7¢ How much did Roberto pay for all the pencils? Darken the circle for the correct answer. If the correct answer is not given, darken the circle for *NH, not here.***

Allow students time to find and mark their answer.

SAY: **You should have darkened the circle for *B, 77¢,* because *11 x 7 = 77.***

Check to see that all students have filled in the correct answer spaces. Ask students if they have any questions.

SAY: **Now you will finish the test on your own. Read the directions carefully. Then do questions 1 through 22 just as we did the samples. Darken the circle for each correct answer, or write in your answer. If the correct answer is not given, darken the circle for *NH, not here.* When you come to the arrow and the words *GO ON* at the bottom of a page, continue working on the next page. When you come to the stop sign at the bottom of page 117, put your pencils down. You have 25 minutes to complete the test. You may now begin.**

Allow students 25 minutes to find and mark their answers.

9 $\begin{array}{r} 57 \\ \times 9 \\ \hline \end{array}$

| | | | | |
|---|---|---|---|---|
| 4563 | 453 | 456 | 156 | NH |
| Ⓐ | Ⓑ | Ⓒ | Ⓓ | ● |

10 $50 \times 2 = \square$

| | | | | |
|---|---|---|---|---|
| 10 | 52 | 70 | 100 | NH |
| Ⓕ | Ⓖ | Ⓗ | ● | Ⓚ |

11 $\begin{array}{r} 10 \\ \times 64 \\ \hline \end{array}$

| | | | | |
|---|---|---|---|---|
| 74 | 110 | 604 | 640 | NH |
| Ⓐ | Ⓑ | Ⓒ | ● | Ⓔ |

12 $\begin{array}{r} 123 \\ \times 4 \\ \hline \end{array}$

| | | | | |
|---|---|---|---|---|
| 462 | 472 | 492 | 592 | NH |
| Ⓕ | Ⓖ | ● | Ⓙ | Ⓚ |

13 $5\overline{)35}$

| | | | | |
|---|---|---|---|---|
| 5 | 6 | 7 | 8 | NH |
| Ⓐ | Ⓑ | ● | Ⓓ | Ⓔ |

14 $36 \div 6 = \square$

*6*

15 **Sally bought a bunch of balloons for $3.59. She paid $0.27 tax. How much did she pay altogether for the balloons?**

| | | | | |
|---|---|---|---|---|
| $3.36 | $3.72 | $3.76 | $3.82 | NH |
| Ⓕ | Ⓖ | Ⓗ | Ⓙ | ● |

16 **Harbor Hills Elementary School has 789 students. What is that number rounded to the nearest hundred?**

**789**

| | | | | |
|---|---|---|---|---|
| 700 | 750 | 790 | 800 | NH |
| Ⓐ | Ⓑ | Ⓒ | ● | Ⓔ |

17 **Amy saw 62 cars in one train. What is that number rounded to the nearest ten?**

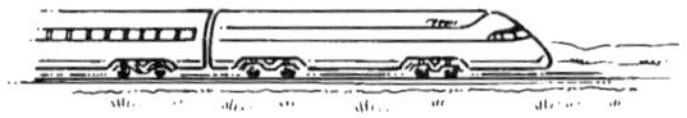

| | | | | |
|---|---|---|---|---|
| 50 | 60 | 65 | 70 | NH |
| Ⓕ | ● | Ⓗ | Ⓙ | Ⓚ |



GO ON

Sample B

Roberto bought 11 pencils. Each pencil cost 7¢. How much did Roberto pay for all the pencils?

| 18¢ | 77¢ | 87¢ | 88¢ | NH |
|---|---|---|---|---|
| Ⓐ | ● | Ⓒ | Ⓓ | Ⓔ |

STOP

18 It takes the juice from 3 oranges to make a full glass of orange juice. Ed wants to make 5 glasses of juice. How many oranges does Ed need?

| 15 | 12 | 10 | 8 | NH |
|---|---|---|---|---|
| ● | Ⓑ | Ⓒ | Ⓓ | Ⓔ |

19 Fay made a list of all the toy animals she owns.

| Mice | Bears | Dogs |
|---|---|---|
| 15 | 3 | 9 |

How many toy animals does Fay own altogether?

| 12 | 18 | 24 | 27 | NH |
|---|---|---|---|---|
| Ⓕ | Ⓖ | Ⓗ | ● | Ⓚ |

20 Noriko cut 46 fabric squares for a quilt. There were 18 striped squares. The rest were solid colors. How many solid-colored squares did Noriko cut?

● 28

Ⓑ 38

Ⓒ 63

Ⓓ 64

Ⓔ NH

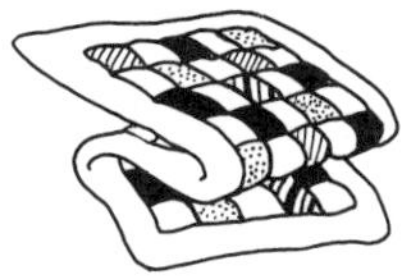

21 Fran wants to buy this purse that costs $10.00. She has $2.50. How much more money does she need to buy the purse?

| $7.50 | $7.75 | $8.25 | $8.50 | NH |
|---|---|---|---|---|
| ● | Ⓖ | Ⓗ | Ⓙ | Ⓚ |

22 A group of 561 adults and 804 children went to the circus. How many more children than adults went on the outing?

| 343 | 333 | 243 | 233 | NH |
|---|---|---|---|---|
| Ⓐ | Ⓑ | ● | Ⓓ | Ⓔ |

STOP

117



SAY: **It is now time to stop. You have completed Part 2 of Practice Test 3. Make sure you have carefully filled in your answer spaces and have completely erased any stray marks. Then put your pencils down and close your books.**

After the test has been scored, review the questions and answer choices with students. If students are having difficulty, provide them with additional practice.

UNIT TWELVE

# Practice Test 4

## Listening

**Sample A**

Ⓐ depressing
● encouraging
Ⓒ frightening
Ⓓ upsetting

STOP

**For questions 1–12, darken the circle for the word or words that best complete the sentence you hear.**

1 Ⓐ tiny Ⓑ main ● huge Ⓓ important

2 Ⓕ teenager Ⓖ student Ⓗ boss ● worker

3 Ⓐ excite ● create Ⓒ ruin Ⓓ scatter

4 ● trick them Ⓖ help them Ⓗ teach them Ⓙ harm them

5 Ⓐ admire ● achieve Ⓒ rest Ⓓ discuss

6 Ⓕ common Ⓖ surprising Ⓗ pretend ● grand

7 Ⓐ birthday ● holiday Ⓒ weekday Ⓓ school day

8 Ⓕ draw a straight line Ⓖ wander around Ⓗ slide down something ● run very fast

9 Ⓐ dress Ⓑ coat Ⓒ snowsuit ● hat

10 Ⓕ bargain Ⓖ settlement ● disagreement Ⓙ discussion

11 Ⓐ solid Ⓑ narrow ● empty Ⓓ overflowing

12 ● freedom Ⓖ slavery Ⓗ responsibility Ⓙ duty

STOP

118



# Practice Test 4: Listening

Allow 20 minutes for this test.

Distribute scratch paper to students. Tell them they may use the scratch paper to take notes while you are reading the passage to them.

SAY: **Turn to Practice Test 4, Listening, on page 118.**

Check to see that all students find Practice Test 4.

SAY: **In this test you will use your listening skills to answer questions. This test is divided into two parts. For each part there is a sample exercise. We will work each sample together. Look at Sample A. In this part of the test, you will choose words that best complete sentences. Listen carefully. I will read part of a sentence and four answer choices. You will find the word or words that best complete the sentence. Keesha felt upbeat after the speaker's positive message. Positive means— A *depressing* …B *encouraging* …C *frightening* …D *upsetting.***

Allow students time to find and mark their answer.

SAY: **You should have darkened the circle for *B, encouraging,* because *positive* means *encouraging.***

Check to see that all students have filled in the correct answer space. Ask students if they have any questions.

SAY: **Now you will choose more words or groups of words that best complete sentences. Find number 1. We will do numbers 1 through 12 just as we did Sample A. Listen carefully to the sentence and the four answer choices. Then darken the circle for the correct answer.**

1 **There was a tremendous boulder at the cave entrance. Tremendous means— A *tiny* …B *main* …C *huge* … D *important.***
2 **Grandpa was an employee of that company for 20 years. An employee is a— F *teenager* …G *student* …H *boss* … J *worker.***
3 **Carl wants to compose a poem. To compose means to— A excite …B create …C ruin …D scatter.**
4 **Some ads try to deceive people. To deceive someone is to— F *trick them* …G *help them* …H *teach them* …J *harm them.***
5 **They want to accomplish their goal this week. To accomplish means to— A *admire* …B *achieve* …C *rest* … D *discuss.***

UNIT TWELVE

# Practice Test 4

## Listing

**Sample A**

- Ⓐ depressing
- ● encouraging
- Ⓒ frightening
- Ⓓ upsetting

STOP

**For questions 1–12, darken the circle for the word or words that best complete the sentence you hear.**

1. Ⓐ tiny Ⓑ main ● huge Ⓓ important
2. Ⓕ teenager Ⓖ student Ⓗ boss ● worker
3. Ⓐ excite ● create Ⓒ ruin Ⓓ scatter
4. ● trick them Ⓖ help them Ⓗ teach them Ⓙ harm them
5. Ⓐ admire ● achieve Ⓒ rest Ⓓ discuss
6. Ⓕ common Ⓖ surprising Ⓗ pretend ● grand
7. Ⓐ birthday ● holiday Ⓒ weekday Ⓓ school day
8. Ⓕ draw a straight line Ⓖ wander around Ⓗ slide down something ● run very fast
9. Ⓐ dress Ⓑ coat Ⓒ snowsuit ● hat
10. Ⓕ bargain Ⓖ settlement ● disagreement Ⓙ discussion
11. Ⓐ solid Ⓑ narrow ● empty Ⓓ overflowing
12. ● freedom Ⓖ slavery Ⓗ responsibility Ⓙ duty

STOP





6 **The castle was a magnificent structure. Magnificent means— F *common* …G *surprising* …H *pretend* …J *grand.***

7 **Last summer my family took a vacation. A vacation is a— A *birthday* …B *holiday* …C *week day* …D *school day.***

8 **Rita will dash to the finish line. To dash means to— F *draw a straight line* …G *wander around* …H *slide down something* …J *run very fast.***

9 **Her baby wore a pink bonnet. A bonnet is a kind of— A *dress* …B *coat* …C *snowsuit* …D *hat.***

10 **Let's avoid a quarrel. A quarrel is a— F *bargain* … G *settlement* …H *disagreement* …J *discussion.***

11 **We looked in the hollow log. Hollow means— A *solid* … B *narrow* …C *empty* …D *overflowing.***

12 **Many people want to live in a country with liberty. Liberty is— F freedom …G slavery …H responsibility …J duty.**

SAY: **Now go to page 119.**

Sample B

Ⓐ hammer
● flashlight
Ⓒ sandwich
Ⓓ radio

STOP

**For questions 13–24, listen to the story. Then darken the circle for the word or words that best answer the question.**

13 Ⓐ "Sleeping and Playing"
Ⓑ "Kenji and His Playpen"
Ⓒ "A Visit from Japan"
● "An Older Brother's Problem"

14 Ⓕ loud
Ⓖ tiny
● cute
Ⓙ smart

15 Ⓐ became tired
Ⓑ liked the turtle
Ⓒ stumbled and fell
● ran off to play

16 Ⓕ never
Ⓖ in the mornings
Ⓗ in the evenings
● in the afternoons

17 Ⓐ football
Ⓑ basketball
Ⓒ tennis
● baseball

18 Ⓕ California
● Hawaii
Ⓗ Chicago
Ⓙ Texas

19 Ⓐ sail on a boat
● ride in a car
Ⓒ fly in a plane
Ⓓ take a helicopter ride

20 ● grandparents
Ⓖ parents
Ⓗ best friends
Ⓙ aunt and uncle

21 Ⓐ shopping
● on a sleigh ride
Ⓒ ice-skating
Ⓓ to roast marshmallows

22 Ⓕ angry
Ⓖ scared
● proud
Ⓙ worried

23 ● a flag
Ⓑ a window
Ⓒ the door
Ⓓ another tower

24 Ⓕ floor
Ⓖ lawn
● beach
Ⓙ sidewalk

STOP

119



Check to see that all students find Sample B on page 119.

SAY: **Look at Sample B. In this part of the test, you will choose words and phrases that best answer questions about paragraphs and stories that you hear. I will read a story and then ask a question. You will choose the best answer to the question. Listen carefully. Sometimes during heavy thunderstorms, the electricity stops working. One night, during a storm, the lights at Ronald's house went out. Ronald was very nervous. Ronald's father told him not to worry, and went down to the basement.**

**Now look at Sample B. Listen carefully. Then darken the circle for the correct answer. Ronald's father went to the basement to get a— A *hammer* ...B *flashlight* ...C *sandwich* ...D *radio.***

Allow students time to find and mark their answer.

SAY: **You should have darkened the circle for *B*, *flashlight*, because Ronald's father went to the basement to get a *flashlight* so they would be able to see.**

Check to see that all students have filled in the correct answer space. Ask students if they have any questions.

SAY: **Now you will choose more words and phrases that best answer questions to paragraphs and stories that you hear. Find number 13. We will do numbers 13 through 24 just as we did Sample B. Listen carefully to the story and question. Then darken the circle for the correct answer.**

**Listen as I read this story. You will answer two questions.**

**After Kenji was born, Grandma came to visit from Japan. She met my new brother Kenji for the first time. Everyone in my family likes Kenji because he is so cute. They talk about him all day. I like him too, but I want my family to like me again. I came first. I am nine years old. I have a lot to talk about. Kenji cannot talk. He just sleeps in his crib or plays in his playpen all day.**

13 **What would be a good title for this story? A *"Sleeping and Playing"* ...B *"Kenji and His Playpen"* ...C *"A Visit from Japan"* ...D *"An Older Brother's Problem."***

14 **Everyone likes Kenji because he is so— F *loud* ...G *tiny* ...H *cute* ...J *smart.***

Now put your finger on number 15. Listen carefully as I read this story. You will answer one question.

Manuel told Larry that his turtle could beat Larry's dog in a race. Larry didn't believe him, so they decided to see what would happen. The dog ran very fast, and the turtle crawled very slowly. But just before the dog reached the finish line, he saw another dog and ran off to play with it. The turtle kept crawling until he reached the finish line.

15 The dog didn't finish the race because he— A *became tired* ...B *liked the turtle* ...C *stumbled and fell* ...D *ran off to play.*

Now put your finger on number 16. Listen carefully as I read this story. You will answer two questions.

Everyone enjoys Whitehall Park. In the mornings, mothers and fathers spend time there, pushing their babies in strollers. During the afternoons, young children play on the swings and slides. In the evenings, older children play baseball.

16 Young children play in Whitehall Park— F *never* ...G *in the mornings* ...H *in the evenings* ...J *in the afternoons.*

17 Older children use the park to play— A *football* ...B *basketball* ...C *tennis* ...D *baseball.*

SAY: Now put your finger on number 18. Listen carefully as I read this story. You will answer two questions.

Mr. and Mrs. Hiroshi live in Chicago. They are excited because they are going on a trip. First, they will drive their car to the airport. Then they will fly in a plane to California. From there they will sail on a boat to Hawaii. In Hawaii, they will take a helicopter ride to see parts of the islands.

18 Mr. and Mrs. Hiroshi are going on a trip to— F *California* ...G *Hawaii* ...H *Chicago* ...J *Texas.*

19 The first thing they will do is— A *sail on a boat* ...B *ride in a car* ...C *fly in a plane* ...D *take a helicopter ride.*

Now put your finger on number 20. Listen carefully as I read this story. You will answer two questions.

Neil and his grandparents went to Vermont this winter. Neil's grandparents took him on a horse-drawn sleigh ride. His cousins took him ice-skating on the pond. They roasted marshmallows in the fireplace. Neil had a good time in Vermont.

20 Neil went to Vermont with his— F *grandparents* ... G *parents* ...H *best friends* ...J *aunt and uncle.*

21 Neil's grandparents took him— A *shopping* ...B *on a sleigh ride* ...C *ice-skating* ...D *to roast marshmallows.*

Now put your finger on number 22. Listen carefully as I read this story. You will answer three questions.

Tara and Matthew built a sand castle. They put three towers on their castle. On top of the tallest tower, they put a flag. They put the door on the middle tower. On the smallest tower, they put a window.

22 After building their castle, Tara and Matthew probably felt— F *angry* ...G *scared* ...H *proud* ...J *worried.*

23 On top of the tallest tower, Tara and Matthew put— A *a flag* ...B *a window* ...C *the door* ...D *another tower.*

24 Tara and Matthew are playing on the— F *floor* ... G *lawn* ...H *beach* ...J *sidewalk.*

SAY: It is now time to stop. You have completed Practice Test 4. Make sure you have carefully filled in your answer spaces and have completely erased any stray marks. Then put your pencils down and close your books.

After the test has been scored, review the questions and answer choices with students. If students are having difficulty, provide them with additional practice.

UNIT THIRTEEN

# Practice Test 5

## Language

**Sample A**

**Let's Get a Pet**

Kelly wants to have a pet. She's not sure what kind of pet she wants. Kelly's cousin Maureen has a few pets. Kelly decides to write Maureen a letter to find out which pet she likes best.

**Why is Kelly writing this letter?**

- Ⓐ to find out more about kittens
- ● to help her decide what pet to get
- Ⓒ to help her parents learn more about pets
- Ⓓ to learn to write better letters

STOP

**For questions 1–4, darken the circle for the correct answer, or write in the answer.**

**Kelly found the book *Taking Care of a Pet* in the library. Use part of the Index from this book to answer questions 1 and 2.**

**Index**

aquarium pets
  first aid and diseases, 248–249
beds
  for cats, 33
  for dogs, 21–22
cages
  canaries, 62–63
  hamsters, 54–55
  white mice, 51
first aid, 231–254
rabbits
  cleanliness, 42, 44
  handling, 41–42
  teeth, 44–45

1 **Information about first aid for pets can be found on all these pages except—**

| 232 | 245 | 250 | 260 |
|---|---|---|---|
| Ⓐ | Ⓑ | Ⓒ | ● |

2 **Kelly can find information about cages for white mice on which pages?**

*51*

3 **Kelly put these words in alphabetical (*ABC*) order so she could find them more quickly in the dictionary. Which list is correct?**

- Ⓕ guinea pigs – gerbils – goldfish – guppies
- Ⓖ guppies – guinea pigs – goldfish – gerbils
- Ⓗ guppies – gerbils – goldfish – guinea pigs
- ● gerbils – goldfish – guinea pigs – guppies

4 **Kelly found the book *How to Take Care of a Pet*. Where should she look to find the author's name?**

- Ⓐ Chapter 1
- ● the title page
- Ⓒ the index
- Ⓓ the table of contents

GO ON





# Practice Test 5: Language

Allow 30 minutes for this test.

SAY: **Turn to Practice Test 5, Language, on page 120.**

Check to see that all students find Practice Test 5.

SAY: **In this test you will use the language skills that we have practiced in this unit. Look at Sample A. Read the paragraph entitled "Let's Get a Pet" carefully. Then read the question and the answer choices. Darken the circle for the correct answer.**

Allow students time to find and mark their answer.

SAY: **You should have darkened the circle for *B*, next to *To help her decide what pet to get*. The paragraph states that Kelly is writing to her cousin because her cousin has a lot of pets. Kelly plans to ask her cousin which pet she likes best. Kelly thinks that this information might help her decide what kind of pet she should get.**

Check to see that all students have filled in the correct answer space. Ask students if they have any questions.

SAY: **Now you will finish the test on your own. Do numbers 1 through 27 just as we did Sample A. Read each set of directions and each paragraph carefully. Then read the questions and answer choices carefully. Darken the circle for each correct answer, or write in your answer. For questions 28 through 35, darken the circle for the word that is misspelled. If all the words are spelled correctly, darken the circle for *No mistake*. When you come to the words *GO ON* at the bottom of a page, continue working on the next page. When you come to the stop sign at the bottom of page 128, put your pencils down. You have 30 minutes to complete the test. You may now begin.**

Allow students 30 minutes to find and mark their answers.

**Here is the first part of Kelly's letter. Read it carefully. Then answer questions 5–8.**

Dear Maureen,

How are you doing? **(1)** Are your pets doing well? **(2)** I can get a pet my mom and dad told me. **(3)** Now I need to decide. **(4)** Which one to get. **(5)** My mom and dad bought me a new bicycle. **(6)** I think having a pet will be fun. **(7)** I know it's a big responsibility. **(8)** Mom told me that I would have to take care of it. **(9)** I'll have to give it food and water. **(10)** I'll have to make it comfortable. **(11)** I can't wait to do all this. **(12)** That's why I'm writing to you. **(13)**



**5 The best way to write sentence 3 is—**

- ● My mom and dad told me that I can get a pet.
- Ⓖ My mom told me that I can get a pet, my dad, too.
- Ⓗ A pet my mom and dad told me I can get.
- Ⓙ As it is written.

**6 Which group of words is not a complete sentence? Write the number of the group of words.**

*5*

**7 Which of these sentences could be added after sentence 13?**

- Ⓐ Kittens are fun to have as pets.
- Ⓑ Do you have a new bicycle?
- ● What pet do you think I should get?
- Ⓓ Will you be able to come to my house?

**8 Which sentence does not belong in Kelly's letter?**

| 6 | 7 | 8 | 10 |
|---|---|---|---|
| ● | Ⓖ | Ⓗ | Ⓙ |

GO ON

**Here is the next part of Kelly's letter. This part has groups of words underlined. Read the letter carefully. Then answer questions 9–14.**

There are many pets I'd like to get. I would love to have a kitten
**(14)** **(15)**
a puppy, and a hamster. Dad says I have to choose one. A kitten
**(16)** **(17)**
might be a good pet for me. Kittens love to be cuddled. I would
**(18)** **(19)**
be very gentle with it when I held it. Kittens is very playful. They
**(20)** **(21)**
love to play with little balls and string. Kittens needed to be fed
**(22)**
every day. Do you think an kitten would be a good pet for me?
**(23)**

sincerely yours,
Kelly

**9 In sentence 15, a kitten a puppy, and a hamster. is best written—**

- Ⓐ a kitten a puppy and a hamster.
- Ⓑ a kitten, a puppy and a hamster.
- ● a kitten, a puppy, and a hamster.
- Ⓓ As it is written.

**10 In sentence 17, might be a good pet is best written—**

- Ⓕ a good pet might be
- Ⓖ might a good pet be
- Ⓗ be a might good pet
- ● As it is written.

**11 In sentence 20, Kittens is very is best written—**

- ● Kittens are very
- Ⓑ Kittens were very
- Ⓒ Kittens am very
- Ⓓ As it is written.

GO ON

12 **In sentence 22, needed to be fed is best written—**

Ⓕ needs to be fed

● need to be fed

Ⓗ needing to be fed

Ⓙ As it is written.

13 **In sentence 23, Do you think an kitten is best written—**

Ⓐ Do you thinks an kitten

Ⓑ Do you thinks a kitten

● Do you think a kitten

Ⓓ As it is written.

14 **At the end of Kelly's letter, sincerely yours, is best written—**

Ⓕ Sincerely Yours,

● Sincerely yours,

Ⓗ sincerely Yours,

Ⓙ As it is written.

GO ON

Drew is writing a report on his trip ot Arizona. Read the following. Then answer questions 15–18.

## A Dry Land

Drew's teacher wants the class to write a report about their favorite vacation. Drew enjoyed seeing the desert. So, Drew decided to write his report about his trip to Arizona.

**15 What is the first thing Drew should do before he begins to write his paper?**

Ⓐ Remember what other vacations were like.

Ⓑ Buy books about deserts.

● Make a list of what he saw in the desert.

Ⓓ Ask his sister to write about the desert, too.

**16 If Drew wants to find the meaning of the word cactus, where should he look first?**

Ⓕ an encyclopedia

● a dictionary

Ⓗ a language arts book

Ⓙ an atlas

**17 If Drew wants to learn more about deserts, he should look in—**

● an encyclopedia.

Ⓑ a dictionary.

Ⓒ a newspaper.

Ⓓ a language arts book.

**Before Drew begins his report, he looks up some words in the dictionary.**

**18 What definintion best fits the word dry as used in the sentence below? Write the definition.**

**Some plants grow well in a *dry* climate.**

***having little or no rainfall***

GO ON

Here is the first part of Drew's report. Read it carefully. Then answer questions 19–23.

## Sunny Arizona

We stayed in hotels. (1) We visited during the day many places. (2) We had to drive many miles. (3) Last year we visited Maine. (4) Most of the time we drove through a desert. (5) I couldn't believe how big it was. (6) It is very dry in a desert. (7) It is very sunny in a desert. (8) A place is called a desert. (9) If it gets less than ten inches of rain each year. (10) Staying in a desert makes you thirsty. (11) We made sure that we had plenty of water to drink. (12)

19 **Which sentence would best begin this paragraph?**

- Ⓕ I like to go on vacation.
- ● My vacation to Arizona was so much fun!
- Ⓗ Next year we plan to visit Texas.
- Ⓙ Summer vacation starts in two weeks.

20 **The best way to write sentence 2 is—**

- Ⓐ During the day many places we visited.
- ● During the day we visited many places.
- Ⓒ Many places we visited during the day.
- Ⓓ As it is written.

GO ON

21 **Which sentence does not belong in Drew's report? Write the number of the sentence.**

*4*

22 **Which of these is not a complete sentence?**

| 5 | 7 | 10 | 12 |
|---|---|---|---|
| Ⓕ | Ⓖ | ● | Ⓙ |

23 **What is the best way to combine sentences 7 and 8 without changing their meaning?**

Ⓐ Since it is very sunny it is dry in a desert.

Ⓑ It is very dry in a desert and it is very sunny.

Ⓒ Being very dry it is also very sunny in a desert.

● It is very dry and sunny in a desert.

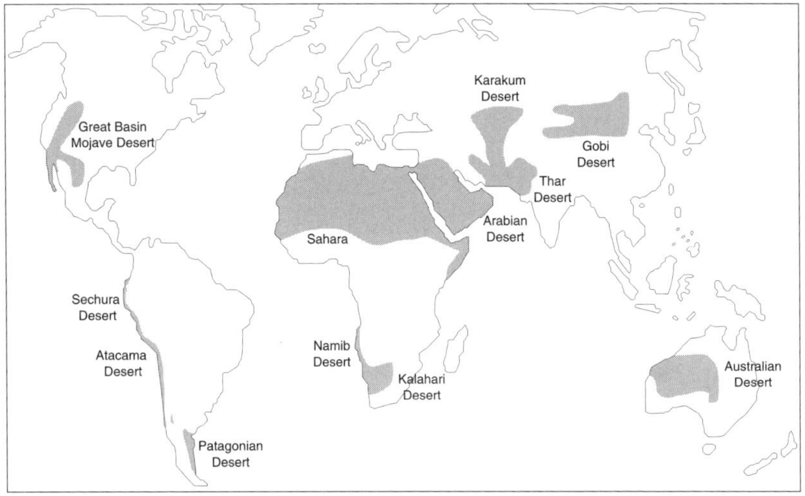

Here is the next part of Drew's report. This part has groups of words underlined. Read the draft carefully. Then answer questions 24–27.

I used to think that an desert was just all sand. **(13)** Some deserts in the world are mostly sand. **(14)** The desert that I saw in Arizona has some interesting plants. **(15)** One plant I saw was the cactus. **(16)** This kind of plant can survive with very little rain. **(17)** I also seen clumps of grass. **(18)** At certain times of the year a Desert does get some rain. **(19)** That's when you can see many colorful flowering plants. **(20)** I think the desert was a very interesting place to visit. **(21)** I hope I can visit it again someday. **(22)**

**24 In sentence 13, that an desert is best written—**

Ⓕ that a deserts

Ⓖ that an deserts

● that a desert

Ⓙ As it is written.

**25 In sentence 18, I also seen is best written—**

● I also saw

Ⓑ I also see

Ⓒ I also sees

Ⓓ As it is written.

**26 In sentence 19, a Desert does get is best written—**

Ⓕ a desert do get

● a desert does get

Ⓗ a Desert do get

Ⓙ As it is written.

**27 In sentence 22, I can visit it again is best written—**

Ⓐ I cans visit it again

Ⓑ i can visit it again

Ⓒ I, can visit it again

● As it is written.

GO ON

For questions 28–35, read each sentence carefully. If one of the words is misspelled, darken the circle for that word. If all the words are spelled correctly, then darken the circle for *No mistake.*

28 The children laughd at the circus clowns. No mistake
● Ⓖ Ⓗ Ⓙ

29 We watched the snow falling on the mowntan. No mistake
Ⓐ Ⓑ ● Ⓓ

30 We collected colorful seashells on the beachs of Hawaii. No mistake
Ⓕ Ⓖ ● Ⓙ

31 This apple is sweet and juicy! No mistake
Ⓐ Ⓑ Ⓒ ●

32 The family was able to safly leave the burning house. No mistake
Ⓕ ● Ⓗ Ⓙ

33 The tinyest kitten is black and white. No mistake
● Ⓑ Ⓒ Ⓓ

34 Birds built nests in the branchs of the oak trees. No mistake
● Ⓖ Ⓗ Ⓙ

35 Lynn threw a penny into the wishing well. No mistake
Ⓐ Ⓑ Ⓒ ●

STOP





SAY: **It is now time to stop. You have completed Practice Test 5. Make sure that you have carefully filled in your answer spaces and have completely erased any stray marks. Then put your pencils down and close your books.**

After the test has been scored, review the questions and answer choices with students. If students are having difficulty, provide them with additional practice.